To my longtime
FFF friend

Ben Ferencz

may your world
be as good to you as
mine has been to me

Howard

What a World!
What a Life!
Sequel

Recollections and Reflections
by Howard S. Brembeck

What a World!
What a Life!
Sequel

"You have lived in a century of unprecedented change and you've led a life that has had a lasting effect on others. I think people deserve to hear about your experiences and learn your thoughts."

—Rosalynn Carter

"Every street we traveled and every person we met reminded us of circumstances and events that had shaped our lives, conditioned our thinking and set the stage for the future."

Preface

Having written the first edition of *What a World! What a Life!* just for my family and close friends, I was very much surprised to find out that there were people I didn't even know who wanted copies for their families and friends. Some have requested additional printings or a sequel. I have opted to write a sequel with a different twist—including some material from the previous book and adding new material as well. In this volume I have chosen to sometimes use my native "Hoosier language." My dad used to sing a ditty: "I was born in the town of Wabash when the town was on the bum. They all said that I couldn't live because I was born too young; but my mother rushed the bottle and my dad the can until I became a man." I don't know whether he was talking about himself or me! Being young was no problem—I outgrew that. But I have found that immaturity can last a lifetime, even to ninety-two, so please excuse all immature observations and comments.

—*Howard S. Brembeck*

*"Dad always said that the farm was a
great place for raising boys."*

1

My Early Years

My dad was right about Wabash being on the bum. Located on the canal that followed the Wabash River, Wabash was at one time a larger town than it is today. Wabash was like my dad's description of one of our neighbor boys—he was sure a sharp young fellow, but he never improved.

Grandfather Frederick Brembeck was a tailor and he taught the trade to my father. My mother, Huldah, whose maiden name was Speicher, was the granddaughter of a couple that had emigrated from Switzerland to Urbana, a town even smaller than Wabash. Mother was a good businesswoman, a good pianist and, from time to time, she wrote poetry. She attended business school in Huntington, Indiana, and after graduation took a job as secretary for the Belgian Draft Horse Association in Wabash. Her office was a block from the Beitman & Wolf Department Store where Paul, my dad, worked as a tailor. The two had become acquainted at Oakwood, a church camp on Lake Wawasee, and the proximity of their workplaces in Wabash contributed to a romance that resulted in marriage.

Being a person who wanted to improve himself, Dad quit his tailoring business in Wabash and moved to a farm in Urbana, Indiana, about ten miles from Wabash. It was at the beginning of World War I, farm prices were high, and although he was a tailor he thought he could learn to farm. My Grandpa Speicher always had an extra farm or two, so getting a farm to live on was no problem.

Growing up on a farm in those days was an enriching educational and spiritual experience. When you live on a farm, you get a better understanding of how the Creator operates and how you fit into creation. You see how animals are conceived and born and often you get to help bring a colt or a calf into the world. You are assigned a front row seat on the glories and mysteries of the universe.

You can imagine my surprise, however, when I found that living in the country meant having no electricity, no indoor plumbing, no heat in the bedrooms, and no streetcar nearby to take me downtown. But there were a lot of things on the farm that I liked very much. You could walk for miles in the woods, go fishing in the creek, or ride horses. I also had pet pigeons, pet rabbits and a goat that I could harness to a little wagon. We had buggy horses that we could turn into riding horses and workhorses powerful enough to pull a plow through hard clay or clinging roots. Dad always said that the farm was a great place for raising boys (he eventually had four sons—Winston, Cole, Paul [Bud] and me).

When I was old enough to help, I was expected to share in the work and so were my brothers. We began our agricultural education with simple chores in the barn and barnyard and, by the time we were ten, we were holding the reins and driving the teams of the heavy horses we used to operate our farm equipment. My father always said working on a farm with a team of horses when you are only ten years old helps you grow up. Without question, I agree. When I was ten and began working a team of horses in the fields, my life was mostly work with very little time for play or for the hunting and fishing that I had come to enjoy.

We four were immersed in the rhythm and routine of the farm. I don't recall that we ever felt overworked, underprivileged or poor, but I must confess that we did envy the kids in town who didn't have to do dawn-to-dusk farm work or endless chores. There certainly was plenty of work to do. From 5 a.m. to 7 p.m. or later and from Monday through Saturday, Dad was plowing, planting, cultivating, mowing, taking care of the livestock or performing other tasks that never seemed to end. On Sunday and in the depth of winter, there was no field work, but chickens and pigs still had to be fed, cows milked and other chores taken care of, responsibilities that required several hours every morning and evening.

At the end of a long work day, if there still was daylight, we often walked to the woods at the back of our farm. We wanted to be among the big trees and to see and hear the birds and animals.

The memories of those moments in the summer twilight have stayed with me over the years. Perhaps that explains my lifelong love of trees and the nature they adorn. Perhaps that's why I've been drawn to visit and revisit Sequoia National Park and other places of great natural beauty.

Imagine with me if you can one of your children racing into the house calling, "Oh Mama, Mama, come quick—there's a car coming down the road." Cars were still a rarity, particularly in the country. Like most other farmers, we had a horse and buggy. I remember well that when we met an automobile coming toward us in our horse and buggy we would stop, pull to the side of the road, and hold the horse by the bridle until the car had passed, for the horses were often frightened by automobiles and wanted to run. Automobiles at that time were very noisy, and horses were unaccustomed to meeting them. I think you too would be frightened to see a buggy coming down the road all by itself, without a horse.

Occasionally, my parents let me stay in town overnight with my friend, Lynn Stark. What a delight not to have chores to do and to have the time to play baseball. My favorite baseball game was what we called "Round-Town." You could work your way from the outfield to the batter's box and you could keep batting as long as you didn't strike out.

We never resented the responsibilities that came with being one of the Brembeck children. Dad didn't believe in doing for people what they could and should do for themselves. He felt that when you help people, you run the risk of retarding their growth toward maturity, possibly preventing them from developing their full capabilities. We were pretty much brought up on the Bible. Dad took it very seriously. In fact, Bible principles were used as practical guides to the way all persons in our family lived their lives and the way they did their work. He helped us understand that everything we do is in God's hands. We plant the crops, but the harvest depends on God.

We were members of the Evangelical Church in Urbana. The church was important to us. In fact, I pledged $400 to the campaign to build a new church building. That was a lot of money in those days, expecially to a young man with limited income and uncertain prospects. But I redeemed my pledge with load after load of sand and gravel that I dug from a creek bed and hauled in a horse-drawn wagon to the building site. It was hard work but I had been taught to keep my word and I was determined to live up to the letter and spirit of that teaching.

The God who watches over us is beyond our understanding, but not beyond our reach. He invites us to come to Him for help. As Jesus reminds us, "Ask and you shall receive; seek and you shall find; knock and it shall be opened onto you."

Many times in my life I've asked for help. I've prayed for the light to know what I should do and how I should do it. The answers always have come—sometimes in ways and at times that were totally unexpected. I'm grateful for the answers but even more grateful that God gave me the good sense to listen to His words and accept the wisdom of His counsel.

Through the years, God has opened many doors for me and He has given me the courage to walk through them into the new worlds of opportunity and challenge that I will now do my best to describe.

2

The People of Urbana

In 1922, my dad bought a Ford Touring Car. This was the biggest investment our family had made except for our home, and although the car was often difficult to start, particularly in cold weather, and one ran the risk of breaking an arm when cranking it, it was a wonderful thing. Instead of knowing only the farm neighbors near us, we now became acquainted with many people two, three or more miles away from us.

Some of our neighbors were real characters. Everybody said that George and Heim Welmon were the smartest people around. George would stand by the railroad and as the freight cars went by he would add the car identification numbers together and claim he could give the total, and people thought he really did have the correct total of all those numbers when the train had passed. And Heim was really book smart. Neither of them ever worked, to speak of. They had their garden, of course, and I think they rented out their fields, but they got by and were respected for their superior intelligence. They would often sit for hours on what we called "the philosopher's bench" at my dad's hardware store, or in the barbershop. They did a lot of reading and could tell you almost anything you wanted to know.

Urbana had two banks, two churches, two grocery stores, a drugstore, a butcher shop, a barber shop, a general store, a jewelry store, a blacksmith shop, the post office and my dad's hardware store. At one time there was also a livery barn where horses and buggies were tied while the owners conducted business in town. I don't think there were more than three to four hundred residents in the entire town, so everybody knew everybody else and almost everything about each other. Those who didn't pay their bills were deadbeats. Those who bummed off of other people were labeled bums, and if anyone stole they were a thief. Dad had a lumber and coal business in addition to the hardware, and some families always stole their coal from Dad's coal pile. People would try to get him to stop the thieves, but he always said if they were so poor that they couldn't afford to pay for the coal he wasn't going to do anything about it. I had the misfortune of having two uncles who were bums. They were experts at bumming off other people, especially their father, and also my mother and dad, so they got through life without working much.

One of the town's characters was Pete Weck, who was very handy at threshing time and would do odd jobs, but never took work seriously. There was one family for whom my mother always felt sorry because they were so poor, but they always seemed to have money for things that we couldn't afford. Then there were the two Freshour families. Willie Freshour, the father of one of the Freshour familes, was the most progressive, up-to-date farmer in our neighborhood. He liked to tell naughty stories (which I noticed made my dad's face turn red when I was present). His stories were good and so was his advice: "Never say what you will do and what you will not do. You will end up doing what you said you wouldn't do and not doing what you said you would." Members of the Charlie Freshour family weren't as ambitious. Once when my dad had bought some corn from Charlie Freshour, we were scooping the corn off the corncrib floor when a rat ran out of the pile. It ran up Charlie's leg, inside his overalls. It got waist high and Charlie was dancing a jig like you have never seen. All my dad and I could do was laugh. He had to take his overalls off to get the rat out.

The Phillip Urschels, our closest neighbors to the east, were a very unusual family. They had nearly everything that a farm family might want, and a lot that we didn't have. They owned a threshing engine and separator and a first-class black percheron stallion. They always had about the best 'coon dogs in the county— usually at least one bloodhound and a blue tick hound. With all due respect to Andrew Lloyd Webber, "the music of the night" isn't only in an orchestra pit. It can be found in the woodlands and the meadows when the hounds are on the trail. They produce a melody of the night like none other. As a boy I loved to go with the 'coon hunters, sometimes not returning home until 2:00 a.m.

The Urshels' watermelon patch was always something to be guarded. Orrville, the Urshels' son near my age, and I would often sleep in a tent with shotguns to keep thieves out of the melon patch at night. Stealing melons was great sport, but I think we changed some people's minds about that when we let go with our shotguns. The father, Phillip, had some strong opinions; he particularly disliked liars, and said that he would have nothing to do with one, because a person who would lie would steal, and a person who would steal would commit murder, and he didn't want to deal with any murderers.

The Urshel family experienced numerous personal tragedies, but they remained cheerful and enjoyed joking. They lost three children in their teens—one son by cancer, one son in an auto accident, and a daughter from an abortion gone badly. In those days it was customary to hold a wake—that is to sit up with a corpse throughout the night, which I did several times. One couldn't visit the Urshels without staying a while. Even though it wasn't mealtime, visitors were always invited to stay for the next meal. They were truly an outstanding family, like none I have seen elsewhere. I have to admit that a lot of times I was envious of Orrville because people of all ages referred to him as "that handsome son of a gun."

For us boys, Saturday night was the big night of the week at Urbana. The town band played in the main square. My dad showed movies on the blank wall of the two-story Macabee Hall across from his store. There was always the prospect that we might be able to walk around the town square enjoying the music of the band with our favorite girl. This, of course, was only on summer nights. During the winter on Saturday night we would slip off to "Rivertown" (Wabash) and play pool for a nickel a game. That was really "sinnin'". On the surface, Urbana seemed to be a very upright, if not holy, place, at least in the daytime. At night there was card playing, euchre, even poker, and, God forbid, even we kids knew there was some hanky-panky going on with some husbands and widows. But all-in-all, Urbana was a wonderful little town in which to grow up, a place where everybody knew you, your parents and your grandparents, and they knew better than you did what kind of a person you were going to be just from your genes.

"Don't blame the ditch."

—An anonymous Indiana farmer

3

Marks of Manhood

When I was fourteen years old, I became a man. Up to that time I had worn black hose with knickers, but when I was fourteen I got a pair of long pants. It was the most prized piece of clothing I had ever possessed. It was also the first time that I had gone threshing. Going threshing was also the mark of a man. I was making a dollar a day! The threshing machine was run by a large, coal-fired steam engine pulling a wide belt over the flywheel on the separator, which usually was fifty feet or more away from the engine. The separator, of course, divided the grain from the straw. A threshing ring was made up of a dozen farmers or more who went from farm to farm helping each other with this heavy work. The farm where they were harvesting provided the dinner, which was traditionally very ample. And, in addition, sometimes they provided cigars. I tried one, but it made me so sick that it was many years later before I ever tried another one.

Once I had the misfortune of upsetting my bundle wagon when coming through the gate of a lane that ran alongside a ditch. Bundle wagons were designed to haul in the sheaves that had been stacked in shocks in the field. One of the wheels of my wagon dropped into the ditch, the wagon turned over, the horses got mixed up in the harness and, needless to say, it was a mess. Fortunately some of the other threshers came to my assistance and helped me get my wagon and horses lined up again. None of them scolded me, but one gave me a bit of advice. "Don't blame the ditch," he said, and I have always remembered that.

Work on the farm was hard. We had nothing but our own muscles and the muscles of our horses. During my years on the farm, we didn't have a tractor. Working in the fields along the road, I saw fancy new automobiles go by, which really took my eye and made me think about getting a good job in the city where I could make more money than I could on the farm. I was inclined toward business even when I was a small child. I created a stockyard with cattle, sheep and pigs—all of which were beautiful stones that I had gathered from the creek. And when I got a little older, I bought some Victor steel animal traps. During the winter I caught a lot of fur-bearing animals, particularly muskrats, which gave me an income of approximately $100. I invested some of my profits in beehives, which produced quite a lot of honey for me and which I sold to the Adam Cook General Store for 25 cents a pound. I also bought some calves at a very low price which I fed and later marketed at a good profit.

I always found doing business to be a lot of fun, but I was now getting old enough that I had to think about what I was going to do after graduating from high school. I thought I would like to go to a big university and learn about economics, but I would have to work awfully hard to earn enough money. Fortunately Dad let me have a team of horses that were not busy during the summertime, which I used to work on road-building, scooping and hauling gravel. For this I got $5 a day for my horses and myself. I would have to work a year to earn enough money to go to the University of Chicago, which I thought had the best school of economics.

In my earlier boyhood days, World War I had made a deep impression on me. I was concerned that my father would have to go to war. My best friend, Claude Wilcox, who played ball with me and allowed me to go hunting with him, was killed in the war.

During the great flu epidemic of the same time period as World War I, it was a custom to separate children so that the highly contagious flu might not take all the children in a family. Since Winston was younger and still a small child, he remained at home with my mother and dad. Most of the summer and fall of 1918, I lived with Herman Blum, a very good friend of my father's who lived about four or five miles from us. He was a bachelor who had come to America as a boilermaker. He lived by himself in a house that was nestled down in a valley along a creek. Herman was my friend. He was a woodsman. He knew all about the animals, the birds, and where to catch the biggest fish. He didn't have an automobile and seldom went to town with his horse and buggy. But Johnny Young, the huckster, came to his house at least once every week. We always got our bread, bologna, Karo syrup and other necessities from Johnny. Herman had a few chickens, from which we got our eggs, and we got our milk from the Hanzelmans up on the hill. For meat we usually killed a chicken or wild rabbit. Fortunately the neighbors in the vicinity butchered rather frequently, so we could also get good, fresh pork or beef from them.

But I must tell you more about the Hanzelmans who lived on the hill. Frequently Herman and I would go to their house in the evening. They were Herman's special friends because they spoke German, and they always had a little something to drink while we were playing checkers. For me it was cider, but for Herman it was something a little more—and this was during prohibition. One of the saddest days in the life of the Hanzelmans was the day the revenuers came and poured all of the wine they had distilled (they had barrels of it in their basement) down the hillside. I can still see Roy, the father, and Jakey, his son, sitting on the hillside with tears running down their faces watching their good wine run down the hillside. At the time I didn't really appreciate the Hanzelmans' position, but as I think about it now, for people who had been drinking wine all their lives, to see all of their efforts poured down the hillside and having to pay a fine on top of their loss seems like a terrible injustice.

Herman's other closest neighbor was Ernie Wilcox, a real woodsman—a hunter, trapper and fisherman. One day while sitting on the bank fishing in Silver Creek, Ernie walked across the nearby bridge and shot his rifle into the water where we were fishing. He then asked me to pull up my line and, sure enough, he had shot my fishing line in two. What a shot! I was so impressed that I wasn't upset about losing my hook and bait. He took me hunting and helped to refine my marksmanship in shooting a bird on the wing or a rabbit on the run with a rifle. He was a real sport. He would never use a shotgun. He said using a shotgun didn't give the animal a fair chance.

The war finally ended and so did the flu epidemic, and it was time for me to go back home. I did so with some reluctance because I enjoyed Herman's company, his stories and his cooking. I still sometimes long for his fried potatoes with onions and bacon. Sometimes we ate raw potatoes. I can tell you that they are not at all bad if the potatoes are fresh and you put a bit of salt on them. There are a few other things I will always remember about Herman. The first thing he did in the morning after getting up was to go out on the porch and yell at the top of his voice. The neighbors were all far enough away that no one could hear him. Second, he would pump himself a glass of cold, fresh water from the well close to the porch. And I never will forget his garden vegetables. He was a very good gardener. I particularly liked his kohlrabi and tomatoes. After I returned home, my dad told me that Herman had cancer in his bowels, so big that they didn't want to operate, and he probably only had a month or two to live. It was summertime, and with Dad's help we pitched a tent on Long Lake where Herman could live out his few remaining days. I took him fishing every day that I stayed with him, and he always insisted on cleaning and frying the fish that we caught. The time came when he had to go to the hospital, and it was there that I saw him die. Two of my very good friends, Claude Wilcox and Herman Blum, had now gone to their happy hunting ground.

Grandpa Speicher had a farm up near where Herman Blum lived which was just grazing land, not tillable. He would go around in his horse and buggy from farm to farm to buy cattle to put on this farm. After he had bought some cattle, he would have me (and sometimes Winston) drive them to this farm. It was hard work to keep the cattle on the road, to keep them from going into an open corn field, for example, or down a farm lane. My relationship with Grandpa Speicher was not very good. He was a very taciturn, quiet fellow who didn't pay much attention to children. I think he paid me something, but not enough to make me like the job. But I did learn something from him, and that was how to dicker—that is, the art of bargaining. As grandpa and I drove around, when we saw cattle that he thought he would like, we would stop and talk to the farmer about buying them. But from the way grandpa talked they weren't very good cattle, the market was bad, and I couldn't see how he and the farmer could ever get together on a price. Yet many times we would drive down the lane and out onto the road, and he would holler, "My last offer—$5 more—that's it. Take it or leave it." And the farmer would often take it. And all the time I was hoping the farmer wouldn't take it, because then I wouldn't have to drive the cattle. I think this experience influenced me away from trying to dicker with a person when buying something.

4

The Real World

A few years later I was thinking about attending the University of Chicago to learn how to become a good economist and businessman so that I could make enough money to buy a beautiful, big car. But things were not good in the city. The stock market had crashed, but I went ahead to the university anyway. I stayed at the Tau Kappa Epsilon house which was just across the street from the home of Alonzo Stagg. He and Knute Rockne were considered the fathers of modern football, and at that time Alonzo Stagg was the coach at the University of Chicago. It was very fortunate for us because the Staggs invited us over for dinner occasionally. They were fine people and had two sons who were very good athletes.

Robert Maynard Hutchen was the new president of the University of Chicago, and he had ideas which he tried to instill in all his students about higher education. For a farm boy the University of Chicago was a great experience. I was fairly familiar with the city of Chicago, but of course had no previous experience with the university. Things went real well in college until I got word that the bank in which both my dad and I had all our money had closed its doors. Time proved that it had closed for good, and neither of us ever got a dime of the money we had on deposit. What can you do when you don't have any more money and you can't borrow any? The only thing left to do was pack up and go home, which I did.

After returning home I got a job with International Harvester in Fort Wayne, a large truck manufacturing plant. I took home about $14.75 per week. It really wasn't much of a job—I was the mail handler. I picked up the mail at the post office in the morning—there was usually a large bag, sometimes so heavy I could hardly lift it. I placed it on the streetcar and brought it to the main office, where it was distributed in smaller packages to various individuals throughout the plant. I was responsible to see that each person received his mail. It had some benefits. I had time to watch people in different areas doing their work. I particularly liked to watch the pattern makers. They made nearly everything out of wood, including the engine, as models for the dies that would be used to cast or mold or draw different parts. I got to see nearly every part of that large International Harvester truck plant. I even got to see the president about twice a day when I delivered and picked up his mail. But I was not making much headway financially. After I paid my room and board at the YMCA and went to a movie once or twice a week, I had practically nothing left to show for my week's work.

On weekends, of course, I went home. Mr. D. E. Speicher, my mother's first cousin and the owner of the Cyclone Manufacturing Company in Urbana, Indiana, became aware of my position and told me that if I wanted to learn to become a manufacturer he would teach me, and on top of that would give me $5 a week. This was $5 more than I was gaining at the time, because I would be living with my parents who would provide my food and lodging. It seemed like a good deal, and it was.

5

Becoming a Salesman

Mr. Speicher was true to his word. He taught me everything about the business, from the receiving of steel and all components to making out shipping orders and bills of lading. He also taught me how to operate the machinery—even the typewriter. He taught me to write and fold a letter properly and prepare it for mailing. After a year or two in the plant I became restless and asked if I could become a salesman. I had bought a Model T Ford and I thought it would be interesting to travel to various parts of the United States and find out if I actually could sell poultry equipment. I had never been far from home, and was naïve enough not to know how big the United States was. The fact was, I had never seen a mountain until I arrived in Pennsylvania. But it was a good time of year, and I worked my way up through the "Finger Lakes" region of New York state, and through the Berkshires of Massachusetts, and on up to Portland, Maine, then back down through Boston, Providence, New Rochelle, and the "Big Apple," where we had some good customers. At that time people raised chickens in small quantities, and we had little feeders and waterers that sold very well in stores like Woolworth's, G. C. Murphy, McCrory, etc. Seed stores and pet stores also sold our products. I was trying to find my way around in lower Manhattan when a policeman noticed me and asked what I was looking for. I said I was looking for the Wrigley building. He said, "I'm sorry, young man, to tell you—I think you are in the wrong city. You need to go about a thousand miles west of here. The Wrigley building is in Chicago." Of course I had meant to say the Woolworth building. He was very polite and directed me to the building a block away. He told me that parking along the street was usually not permitted, but since they didn't often have young men from Indiana driving in downtown New York, he would permit me to park there, and he assured me that I did not need to worry about my car.

New York City was a nice place in those days. I ran my Model T up and down Broadway and Park Avenue; I even went over to Brooklyn to visit relatives, then I went out on Long Island and stayed at Southampton over the weekend. It was a rather long weekend, and the first time that I had not been able to stay busy with doing and seeing. Southampton was not a very exciting place to spend a weekend. I went to a movie house which also had live entertainment. They sang "Back Home Again in Indiana," and that did it. I had never thought of what a nice place Indiana was until I went to Southampton that weekend. I regretted not having stayed in New York City where there was plenty of activity all the time.

Working my way down the coast, I came to Philadelphia, and for the second time I had a policeman pull me over. He said, "This is a one-way street." This was so incomprehensible to me— I had never experienced this before—that I said, "I'm only going one way." "But," he said, "please understand. You're going the wrong way." Later I found that there were other one-way streets, and I tried to keep from going the wrong way on them.

Arriving in Philadelphia, I visited Cyclone's number one customer on Market Street, right across from Independence Hall. The owner was a very fine gentleman who had a lot of respect for Mr. Speicher, and he offered to take me through Independence Hall. "You can see the Liberty Bell, and the place where the Constitution of our nation was born." After that he took me to the Crowell Publishing Company for lunch where the *Ladies' Home Journal* and the *Country Gentlemen* were published. I didn't think much about it at the time, but I wonder how many managers of a business would take the time off to escort a salesman through historic places in their city.

We had a small dealer in Keene, New Hampshire, who was quite a good customer. It was getting late in the day when I called on him and he asked where I was going to spend the night. I told him I would find a tourist home. He invited me to stay with him— he was a bachelor with a housekeeper who was a good cook. I stayed and found this to be true. In the evening, however, sitting around and talking, he made a confession to me. He said he'd always wondered about the territory on the other side of the

Hudson River. He said, "Are there many Indians over there now? And, Indiana, I just don't know where it is. Is it on this side or beyond the Mississippi River? Is it close to California?" Although not very smart, he certainly was a kindly old man, and remained a loyal Cyclone dealer for many years.

Back in Boston I had acquired a taste for lobster. The usual price was $1.75 for a lobster dinner. In Philadelphia there was Bookbinders, a famous seafood place where I got another lobster dinner, and later on in Baltimore I ate lobster at the Chesapeake and Ohio Seafood Restaurant, and at Miller's. Taking a ferry to the Eastern Shore, I found how delicious crab and oysters could be. Oysters of all kinds—I particularly liked raw oysters and oyster stew, fried oysters, and oysters Rockefeller. It was now more than two months since I'd left home. In that time I had discovered seafood like I had never dreamed of. I had written a lot of sales, created new customers, and seen mountains and skyscrapers. I had stayed in dozens of tourist homes, and met a lot of fine people, some of which would remain long-time friends. What a world! What a life!

When I returned home, knowing that I had made this trip in a second-hand Model T Ford, people asked me how my car held up. I did change tires and patch inner tubes at least four times during my travels, and several times I took a half day off to work on the engine, tighten the bands on the brakes, and clean up the magneto and spark plugs. In fact, at one point I had to buy complete new bands; coming down the mountain, by the time I got to the bottom I had completely worn out the brake band and reverse band, and the forward band was nearly worn out. All in all, I got along pretty well—no major breakdowns or accidents.

Myra Brembeck

6

Back Home Again, in Indiana for a While . . . and Myra

Back home again in Indiana I worked with Cyclone's engineering department to develop improvements in our product and create new equipment. I was fortunate to get a few patents on some of the new products. But having experienced all the sights of the big cities, particularly New York, Urbana seemed dull by comparison.

On my birthday, February 9, Mary Brane, a schoolmate who had married, invited me to her house for a birthday celebration. She had also invited Myra Bates, whom I had had an acquaintance with for quite a few years through our church, but didn't know very well. My mother always said that I was born on the coldest day of the year, and so it seemed, particularly on this February 9, in 1933. After dinner Mary said they were planning to go to a movie in Wabash. Since it was cold and snowy that February night, I had come prepared. But since their car also did not have heat, Mary gave us a blanket to cover us while riding to the movie. It wasn't a long trip to Wabash but I think this was another of Mary's cupid tricks to get me acquainted with Myra. Under that blanket things began to warm up, and kept warming up all that spring and summer to the point where we were dating every other night, and talking about getting married in December. But fall wasn't far away and I was planning another two-month sales trip. The thought of being away from each other for two months was unbearable. As Cole Porter would say, "Things were too hot to cool down." What could I do? I had always been a rather resourceful fellow, so I came up with a proposal that we get married and she could travel with me on this two-month sales trip. I didn't know what I was asking, and she didn't know when she consented. Love is really blind, but it's also wonderful. We were married in her parents' home on October 3, 1933 and immediately headed east, staying the second night in a tourist home in Mansfield, Ohio where I had stayed before. The next morning I went out to my car and it had a flat tire, so I set out immediately to remove the tire and patch the inner tube. During this time, not knowing what had happened to me, Myra was back in the room having all kinds of thoughts, such as, did I run away and leave her alone after one night? After I finished repairing the tire and returned to the house she hugged me like she never had before. I think this was the only flat tire we had with my newer second-hand car, which was a two-door Model A Ford. It was an excellent little car and we called it "Bony" because I had bought it from a man named Bonewitz.

From Mansfield we went up to Niagara Falls, where we stayed in a tourist home with people that we did not know, but who knew our parents. At first they were a little skeptical about whether we were married, for they had not seen anything about it in the Wabash paper. From Niagara Falls we headed east across New York to the "Finger Lakes" region, where the poultry industry was developing. We stopped to see a professor at Cornell University that I knew. From there we went to Albany, through the Berkshires again, to Hartford and to lower New Hampshire where the broiler industry was really taking off. On this trip I followed very much the same path that I had taken on my previous trip. While I was making my calls, Myra crocheted a tablecloth, which she completed by the time we had finished our trip. It was a beautiful piece of lace. Considering our ignorance of territory and different kinds of people, we got along very well. We did have a problem climbing one of the mountains in New Hampshire. The snow began to fall, and it was slippery enough that we couldn't go any further. We pulled into a little town with about a dozen houses, and talked one of the owners into letting us stay with them for the night. During the night we noticed an old man in our bedroom. I believe we were using his bedroom, and he probably got up in the night, and came to his own bedroom instead of his temporary location.

Myra made friends easily, and often our hostesses would ask her to stay while I was out making calls. So Myra in this way acquired friends with whom she corresponded for years. Staying in tourist homes was quite an experience, both for us and for the hosts who accommodated us. We found some beautiful homes, owned by people who obviously had been quite wealthy and had lost everything except their homes, and had to let out their bedrooms in order to buy food. The good rooms went for $2, ordinary rooms for $1.50. Having never enjoyed prosperity, Myra and I didn't think too much about the depression as long as we had food to eat and a place to stay. This trip was much like my first trip, with a very important exception. Instead of being one we were now two. Myra enjoyed the sights of New York City. We paid only $3.50 for a good hotel room. We often ate at the automat and we took in all the shows we could in the area of Times Square and of course, Radio City Music Hall and Rockefeller Center, which was the big show.

In Norfolk, Virginia we stayed at a very nice place where the lady of the house always called her husband "Precious." Precious didn't play bridge, so Mrs. Precious invited in one of her close friends and we played bridge well into the night with the help of some of her strawberry wine. Our bed was a four-poster canopy which was so high that a step stool was needed to get into it. Although we had planned to move on early in the morning, she asked Precious to go to the grocery store and get some things, and she prepared a real honest-to-goodness southern breakfast—grits, eggs, ham, fruit, etc.

While in Boston walking along the main street we noticed a lady in her car, which was stopped in the middle of the street, arguing with a policeman (that was before the days of traffic lights). As we watched, she got out of the car, slammed the door, stomped over to the sidewalk and just started walking away, leaving her car to argue with the policeman. There were other people with us watching the scene unfolding in the middle of the street, and we all got a big laugh when she slammed the door and walked away from her car.

I was always delighted to go to the Delmarva Peninsula on the Chesapeake Bay. The chicken broiler business had really taken hold in this area, possibly because of Frank Perdue, who was a great promoter of poultry. But that wasn't the only reason I liked

Delmarva. It was seafood paradise—produced the best oysters in the country, and there were also crabs and almost any kind of fish. With my dinner I ordered raw oysters and tried to persuade Myra to eat one of them, but instead of eating one, she got up and left the table. She said, "I just can't stand to look at those slimy things—let alone eat them." And she never did, until our neighbors in Florida, Frank and May Linskey, held one of their annual oyster parties. Each year they would arrange for a shipment of the best, select Maryland oysters. You could have them any way you wanted them. After considerable goading Myra finally swallowed one of the raw oysters, but that was it. Never again. For me, just thinking about Maryland select oysters and soft-shell crab makes my mouth water.

7

At Home in North Manchester

Arriving back in Indiana about Thanksgiving time, we no longer had a place to eat and sleep. What would we do? Stay with our parents? That's what we did for a little while, until Myra's sister, Lois, found a little house for us on Third Street in North Manchester. It was far from luxurious, but in its favor, it had hot water heat and an electric stove. Although it had only one bedroom, one of its best features was that it was only $12.50 per month. Fortunately we both had sets of parents living on farms, where we got milk, eggs, and sometimes a chicken or fresh meat at butchering time.

After tallying up the amount of business I did on our "honeymoon" trip, Mr. Speicher congratulated me and gave me, as I recall, a $4 a week raise.

Working in the factory at Cyclone gave me an understanding of the ordinary blue-collar working man's philosophy, which fashioned my approach to employing people for the rest of my life. I saw a man who was about seventy years old terminated at Cyclone, with nothing to show for his life's work. I don't believe it was because he was unfairly compensated, and admittedly he probably did not think very far ahead, but he never made enough money to save much, and when the time came he could no longer work, he no longer had any future. I determined then that if I was ever an employer I would make sure that when people left my employment they would take something with them—hopefully enough that they would never become destitute.

I really enjoyed working with the fellows in the factory, and I found out about things you normally don't always openly discuss. We had several employees from the hills of Kentucky. I noticed that they made frequent trips back home and when they came back some of our employees made it a point to park close to the cars of those from Kentucky. This was during Prohibition days, so our Kentucky employees were doing a very good sideline business. They gave me a shot and it nearly lifted me off my feet. In good weather we played horseshoes every noon. If you couldn't make a ringer half the time and doubles about a fourth of the time, you didn't have a chance of getting to play much.

Working shoulder-to-shoulder with other blue-collar workers, I got the feeling that they wanted their boss to be able to make money or he could not pay them well. And it has been my experience that they really don't ask for more than what is fair. I don't know that this applies to all in labor, because the unions do push so hard sometimes that businesses are unable to make money and as a consequence they have to let some people go or file bankruptcy.

An Era of Opportunity

We obtained our Eel River home with the help of D. E. Speicher, who always was ready with timely assistance. For two years, we had lived happily in our Third Street home when he told us about a house on the banks of the Eel River, just north of the covered bridge in North Manchester. The house, built by my Uncle Loren, was actually a converted barn located on property owned by my Speicher grandparents. To satisfy unpaid property taxes, the county sheriff was selling the house for $1,100 and D. E. Speicher said he would loan us the money if we needed it.

The house probably was worth the $1,100, but Uncle Loren never built anything very well and so it needed a lot of work. Myra and I spent days repairing and refinishing. We sanded and varnished the floors, papered the walls, painted the woodwork and made dozens of other improvements. When we finished, we couldn't help but feel proud of our little place on the river. It wasn't a mansion by any stretch of the imagination but it was ours. We were in love and simply too naïve to care if we lived in a hut or a palace.

One of the best additions to our home along the Eel River was a little girl named Caryl. I have to agree with Maurice Chevalier—little girls are about the cutest things our Lord ever created. It would be nice if they could stay that way longer, but I guess that wouldn't work. We'd have a world full of cute little girls, but no bathing beauties or mothers or grandmothers.

Myra and I found North Manchester a delightful place to live. We made friends with about a half dozen other couples whose company we enjoyed very much, and with whom we played bridge almost every Sunday night. And there was a group with whom I played poker about every Saturday night. In our bridge group there were three doctors, a funeral director who was also the coroner, the owner of the newspaper, and the owner of the largest drugstore in town. Not much happened in town in which our bridge group did not participate. North Manchester has an exceptionally wide Main Street. All the buildings—business and residential—are well maintained, and the residents are tidy and happy. Manchester College is a wonderful institution; in short, it was and still is a great place to live, particularly if you like to be off the beaten path of the big cities. Myra and I lived in North Manchester for about ten years. Some of this time was during World War II.

Radio Days and Nights

After we moved from the rented house on Third Street in Manchester into a house of our own on Eel River, Mr. Speicher gave us a Philco radio as a kind of housewarming gift. It had a wooden exterior and it was shaped like a Gothic arched window. That radio was our pride and joy for many years. It brought us music, comedy and information. We had a number of favorite programs, and we seldom missed Lowell Thomas reporting the news.

This wasn't my first experience with radio. We had a Crosley at my parents' home that we listened to with earphones and, later, a Magnavox with a loudspeaker. When I was in high school, a friend and I experimented with homemade radios that, thanks to a wire antenna stretched from house to barn, enabled us to listen to one station at a time. If our set was tuned just right and if atmospheric conditions were favorable, we could hear music and news from KDKA in Pittsburgh, WLW in Cincinnati and WLS in Chicago. The music reflected the start of what people now call the "big band era" and it made us eager to attend live performances of orchestras led by such stars as Wayne King, Guy

Lombardo, Benny Goodman and Tommy and Jimmy Dorsey. They were appearing in ballrooms in Chicago and, closer to home, on Lake Wawasee, Syracuse, Indiana, and Lake Manitou, near Rochester, Indiana.

The Philco presented by Mr. Speicher really was more than a wedding/housewarming gift. It was a link with a world that extended far beyond our northern Indiana home territory. It was a one-way version of the internet that, in my most recent years, has connected people across traditions, cultural differences and time zones. Radio, and later television, and now the internet have had an influence that challenges the understanding of those of us who have witnessed the incredibly rapid development of electronic communication.

Our ability to receive and transmit information has expanded at a rate that is beyond belief and I am astounded when I consider how the technology of communication sometimes has leapfrogged ahead of other developments. Take, for example, the advancement to wireless phones. We still use a gas stove, which, although more modern than the one I grew up with, uses basically the same technology. Although the ice box used no electricity or gas then as it does now, depending solely on the periodic delivery of a large block of ice by a very strong iceman, its technological advances also pale in comparison to the strides I've witnessed in communications.

8

Investment Opportunities

One day soon after I was married, a Depression-struck farmer came into the Cyclone office. He was looking for someone who would finance his purchase of three large sows that were about ready to farrow. He needed $300 for the purchase. In return, he promised to pay the person who provided the financing with one 200-pound pig out of each litter. If each sow produced two litters a year, a reasonable expectation, the annual return on the $300 investment would be six 200-pound pigs. I considered the market price for pork and concluded that the farmer was offering a mutually rewarding deal. The only problem was that $300 was all the money I had in the world. But the farmer looked honest and enterprising so I decided to take advantage of the opportunity by giving him my $300. In a matter of months, I was regretting my decision. The price of hogs had plummeted to five cents a pound and my investment appeared to be a monumental mistake.

When I expressed my woes to Mr. Speicher, he responded by saying, "I think now would be a good time to buy more sows." I told him I had already spent all my available money. But he offered more advice. "Why don't you go to your pig man and find out whether he'd like to have three more sows and what they would cost at today's prices."

When I found out that I could finance three more sows for $200, Mr. Speicher offered to give me the money in exchange for a promissory note. So I now was the owner of six sows, each of which was producing two 200-pound pigs for me each year.

My farmer friend was true to his word. He kept all six sows for three years and then asked to be relieved of the agreement. When I went to see the farmer, I was in for a pleasant surprise. He showed me six tremendously large sows and I was able to sell them at a much higher price than I had paid. My principal had increased dramatically and my investment had produced dividends of twelve 200-pound pigs each year for three years.

I didn't know it at the time but, with Mr. Speicher's sage advice, he had given me a lesson in making money through investing. If I had paid attention to the lesson, I would have taken the money I made on the sows and put it into some other good, dividend paying investment and today I might be as rich as Warren Buffett. But like many other people, I used some of my profit on living expenses. I spent my money instead of reinvesting it.

It wasn't long before I regretted my decision to spend rather than invest. I had come to realize that it's a good idea to have two sources of income, one from working and the other from investing. The trick to becoming a successful capitalist is never to spend your investment principal or the dividends it produces on living expenses. Instead, you should think of principal and interest as seed money. Then, depending on your ability to make wise investments, your venture into capitalism will produce lasting, positive results.

As I am writing this Warren Buffett has just bought CTB, the company that I started in 1952. Selling out is no great accomplishment, but it's nice to sell to someone who appreciates a quality company.

Snack Harbor

In the late 1930s I became restless to have a little business of my own, and built a drive-in restaurant in Peru, Indiana. We purchased the necessary equipment and named it Snack Harbor.

I had a friend who had expressed interest in managing Snack Harbor. But after one May-through-September season, he backed out of the deal because he had come to realize that it involved more work than he had expected. So what had started out primarily as an investment turned into another job with Myra, out of necessity, assuming most of the responsibility.

Under her management, Snack Harbor served hamburgers—we called them steakburgers—and other sandwiches, french fries, chicken-in-a-basket, sodas, sundaes, ice cream cones, Cokes and other items. The kitchen staff placed the orders on trays that car-

Snack Harbor, late 1930s

hops delivered to customers seated in their cars while parked on the Snack Harbor lot. Drive-in restaurants were sweeping across the country and Snack Harbor was riding the crest of the wave. The restaurant was busy and, despite the food shortages that developed during the war years and the limitations imposed by gasoline rationing, we were earning a profit.

But there was a problem—the burden Snack Harbor placed on Myra and, to a lesser extent, on me. It wasn't a hobby. It was an all-day job with supplies to order, equipment to operate and employees to deal with. I did help out in the evening after working a full day at Cyclone. I drove to Peru, about twenty miles from Urbana, and pitched in until our midnight closing time. After the doors were locked, there always were dozens of loose ends to tie up so it usually was 1 a.m. or later before we got to bed.

At the time, we were living in our North Manchester home on the Eel River. We liked living there but driving from Peru to North Manchester after working a full day and half the night was a little more than we could take. So we moved to Urbana and, during the Snack Harbor season, we rented a furnished house in Peru.

"During the Depression, the Bechtel store, like many other retail businesses, was forced to close. My father didn't want to see the building stand empty. So despite the fact that he had no experience in hardware retailing, he took over the business and had the name Brembeck & Son painted on the plate glass window."

Paul Brembeck, Howard's father and founder of Brembeck & Son Hardware Store.

9

Life in Urbana

In many ways, we had put down roots in Urbana. Not only did I work long hours at Cyclone but next to the Cyclone office was the Brembeck & Son Hardware Store. The building had been owned by my grandfather, Philip Speicher, and he had rented it to a man named Floyd Bechtel who used it for his hardware business. During the Depression, the Bechtel store, like many other retail businesses, was forced to close. My father didn't want to see the building stand empty. So despite the fact that he had no experience in hardware retailing, he took over the business and had the name Brembeck & Son painted on the plate glass window. When he added the "& Son," I don't think he had any idea which of the four would join him. As it turned out, I had been bitten by the manufacturing bug while Winston and Cole had fallen in love with academia. So that left the youngest brother, Paul, or as most people called him, Bud, to become the "son" in the Brembeck & Son hardware business.

Bud was still in his teens when Dad took over the store, but the two of them made a good team and people liked doing business with them. As a result, the hardware business prospered, eventually selling everything from nuts and bolts to TVs and home appliances and attracting customers from well beyond the little town of Urbana. After Bud came back from the war, he became a full partner with Dad. That made it easier for Dad to have a career in politics. He was a personable man and everybody seemed to like him so it wasn't surprising when he was elected a County Commissioner and then a Republican member of the Indiana General Assembly.

While living in Urbana we had a next-door neighbor, Lowell McLaughlin, who worked for Cyclone, and he liked to do experimental development work. He worked with Jessie who was a

Kentuckian. They made a good pair; in Lowell's basement, they worked on projects of which I had no knowledge. After dinner one evening I went to visit Lowell and his wife, Mary. I had no more than sat down until Mary began calling Lowell "Little Jesus." I tried to get her to tell me why she was calling him that, but she wouldn't tell me. She said Lowell could tell me, but he was just as reluctant as she was to give me information about that name. Slowly the fog cleared. This was at the beginning of the war, when the German submarines were sinking our cargo vessels all along the East Coast daily. President Roosevelt was admonishing everyone to work harder at finding ways to stop this loss. Slowly Lowell began to tell me what he and Jessie had been doing. He said they had developed a flotation device similar to a snowshoe, except it was air-filled, to permit walking on water. He and Jessie had tested it at Long Lake, a few miles from Urbana. Jessie had put on his "water shoes," stepped over the edge of the boat into the water, and his feet went up; Lowell had to dive in to keep him from drowning. Neither of them had ever seen an ocean. Mary interrupted and said, "I don't think you're ever going to get a medal from President Roosevelt for your idea." Lowell said, "Just suppose it would have worked. The sailors on all these ships that have been going down could strap on the water shoes and walk home." At this point, I couldn't keep from laughing, and after I told Myra about it, I think it was a couple of hours before we stopped laughing. For several years after that, employees at Cyclone called Lowell "Little Jesus."

Work at Cyclone was always ten hours a day, six days a week. We began working an extra five hours in the evening. I often came in for the evening shift so, except for Sundays, I didn't have much time at home. And the situation got worse when the United States became involved in World War II. My title at the time was plant superintendent and one of my responsibilities was to help carry out the conversion of our operations from the manufacture of poultry equipment to the production of materials required by our armed forces.

We were ordered by the government to discontinue the use of steel in most of the items in our product line. Instead, we served as a subcontractor to Magnavox Corporation and made machine gun parts, radio chassis and field telephone boxes. The changeover from agricultural products to military items provided valuable experience for me. Before the war, we worked within certain production tolerances. Precision was desirable but not an absolute necessity. But I soon found out that in making machine gun parts, there were no tolerances, only absolutes.

I learned many production lessons. For example, in drawing aluminum of the type and depth needed for field telephone boxes you first had to cool it to a temperature of approximately zero degrees. Without cooling the aluminum, it would have been ruptured by the heat of the drawing process.

In nearly every phase of our war production effort, we ran into difficulties and challenges. But with the help of Mike Hahnert, one of the best tool and die specialists I have known, we generally succeeded in overcoming the obstacles. We met the specifications and Cyclone became one of the country's leading suppliers of the items we were producing.

But our war-focused production didn't keep our plant fully occupied and it certainly did nothing to satisfy the continuing demand for our poultry equipment. So we had to improvise. We substituted a wood-based material called masonite for steel in our poultry feeding troughs and electric brooders. We had glass waterers manufactured for us. To keep Cyclone on track, we also coped with a daunting array of wartime government regulations and with the rationing of fuel and materials.

At the time, I didn't think we were doing anything unusual. The nation was making an all-out push to win the war and extraordinary effort was commonplace. But as I look back on those war years from the vantage point of today, I can hardly believe we accomplished as much as we did in such a short period of time. Clearly, we demonstrated that you never know what you can accomplish until you make an all-out effort.

The war affected my personal as well as my business life. My brother Paul (Bud), a pilot, promptly enlisted in the Air Force. My brother Winston was drafted into the army and served in the Pacific. Although I was almost beyond the age of eligibility for the draft, I passed a physical examination and was classified "A1." However, I was the superintendent of a plant producing war materials and Mr. Speicher persuaded the draft board that he needed me. As a result, I was never called and, while I was willing to join my brothers and millions of other Americans in active military service, I confess I was not unhappy about the opportunity to contribute to the war effort on the home front. While some items—sugar, shoes, tires and gasoline, for instance—were rationed, the hardships of civilian life were nothing compared to those experienced by the men and women serving in the military.

One especially important reason why it was nice to stay home with Myra instead of marching off to war was our daughter, Caryl. She was born in 1938 and it was a delight to be able to watch our cute little girl take her first steps toward growing up rather than be halfway around the world.

While Dad was enjoying success in retailing and in government, my future at Cyclone seemed far less promising. I wanted to improve my position and my income and D. E. Speicher was kind enough to point out the obstacles that faced me at Cyclone. He confided that his family did not want to share ownership with anyone outside the family circle. He said that if he were in my shoes, he probably would be thinking about other employment. Fortunately, I already had an offer. When it became obvious that the war was winding down, a man named Carl Cue came to see me. He was from United Cooperatives in Alliance, Ohio, a firm created to serve the needs of a number of midwestern farmer cooperatives. He said he was searching for a man to head the United Cooperatives hardware department, a position that also involved the management of a barn equipment plant. He thought my experience in manufacturing and purchasing—at the time, I was both Cyclone's plant superintendent and purchasing agent—made me an ideal candidate for the job.

From the time she heard about my offer from United, Myra seemed interested. Then after Carl Cue came to visit us in our home in Urbana, she was sold. She thought we should take advantage of this new opportunity. Caryl soon would be starting her school years and Myra rightly felt it was time for us to get off the Cyclone-Snack Harbor treadmill and head in a direction that seemed to offer more potential in terms of both professional and family life. When it came to thinking about the future of our little family, Myra clearly was ahead of me.

When I told Mr. Speicher about my offer from United and mentioned that it called for a salary of more than twice what I was earning at Cyclone, he encouraged me to take the job. He appreciated the contributions I had made to Cyclone but he also knew his company was limited in what it could offer me in the future. As always, he was gracious in wishing me every success in the years ahead.

For as long as he lived, I had a warm spot in my heart for Mr. Speicher. I went to see him often, especially after I established my own poultry equipment business. He seemed to like the idea that I had gone into business for myself, even though my company was in competition with his. He sounded like a father when he'd ask how many people we were employing and whether or not we were making any money. Once in a while, like a father, he would offer counsel and advice. About a year before his death, I visited with him for the final time. My company, Chore-Time, was really making progress and, when I told him we now employed hundreds of people and shared with him the good news of our profits, he smiled and offered congratulations that clearly came from his heart.

The investment he had made in me had paid off. And I don't think there is any greater satisfaction than seeing a return on an investment that you have made in others or in experiencing the return on an investment others have made in you. D. E. Speicher, my mentor, my friend, my teacher and one of the kindest and gentlest men I shall ever know, died at the grand old age of ninety-eight.

Selling Snack Harbor

After accepting a position with United Cooperatives at Alliance, Ohio, we decided to sell Snack Harbor. A couple from Fort Wayne who had been in the hotel and restaurant business offered us the best price, and told us that they would give us the money when we passed through Fort Wayne on our next trip from Urbana to Alliance. In those days we were very careful not to spend any unnecessary time on the road because gasoline and tires were still hard to get as a result of the war. Our prospective buyers seemed a little cautious about where we would meet to finalize the transaction, and we were a little cautious. We were surprised when they gave us the full amount of the purchase price in cash— mostly $500 bills, and several $1,000 bills, and of course quite a few $100 bills, totaling about $7,000. We no more than left them until we tried to find places in our car, near the seats, to hide some of the money. Driving on toward Alliance, we became more and more nervous about all the cash. Possibly they had gone ahead of us and would try to reclaim the money by force. As we approached Alliance we noticed a car parked with its lights shining right on us, and a couple of people got out of the car and tried to hail us. We felt sure they were robbers. But they drove on ahead of us and then pulled in front, blocking us. Even though they were uniformed, we were frightened because we had not stopped when they had hailed us. They took us directly to the police station in Alliance and advised me that they would take my wife and daughter and her dog home, but I would have to spend the night in jail or post a $60 bond. At that point $60 didn't seem like very much. When I told Carl Cue, my new supervisor at United Cooperatives about my experience, he became very agitated with the police and confronted them. But I didn't get my $60 back, because I had run a stop sign and failed to stop when they hailed me. The rest of the story, however, is that when I took the money to the bank the next day, they were very suspicious. They said they would take the cash, but would not give me credit for it until I had proven to them that this was honest money. As far as I was concerned it was honest money, but there wasn't any doubt at this point that the people who gave it to us had never reported it as income. There was a lot of black market trading occurring at that time in food and other necessities that were rationed.

But our Snack Harbor problems were not yet over. The Internal Revenue Service charged us with violations for not declaring as income food that we had eaten at Snack Harbor. The IRS agent's name was Mr. Colorado. He was a nice person, and I believe he was actually sympathetic toward us, but as he said, it was his job. We would have to think back and determine just how much the two of us had eaten at Snack Harbor. We tried to reconstruct it, but before we got all the information together we received word that Mr. Colorado had died. We expected that someone else would pursue the issue, but thank the Lord (or maybe Mr. Colorado) no one ever did.

10

Launching a Business and Saying Farewell

Breaking up housekeeping in Urbana and ending my career with Cyclone were sobering, even shocking, experiences. During our years in Urbana, we enjoyed the small town atmosphere and, most of all, the comfort of being near family and friends. Every day, we were surrounded by familiar faces and places. Every street we traveled and every person we met reminded us of circumstances and events that had shaped our lives, conditioned our thinking and set the stage for the future.

In Alliance, we faced a new and different experience. We were much more on our own, but we certainly weren't apprehensive. We knew we had been given a great opportunity and we were determined to make the very best of it.

One of the first problems we faced was housing. It was 1945, and the homebuilding industry was a casualty of the war, but returning veterans of the armed forces were helping to create a sky-rocketing demand for new homes. In Alliance and cities across the country, housing was in extremely short supply. So Myra, Caryl and I considered ourselves fortunate when we located a home we could rent for $55 per month. It was adequate but far from luxurious. Because we paid for a number of improvements, the owner kept the rent at $55 through the eight years we spent in Alliance. During those same years, Myra and I started saving money to build a home of our own. We didn't know where it would be built or when we would build it. We only knew that when the time was right, we would have at least some of the money we needed.

At United Cooperatives, I found myself rubbing shoulders with many of the legends of the farm cooperative movement. The board of directors included such men as Harvey Hull, founder of the Indiana Farm Bureau; Clark Brody, founder of Michigan Farm Bureau Services; Cy Vance, one of the founders and the president of Ohio Farm Bureau; Fred Herndon, founder of Illinois Farm Supply, now known as Landmark; and Misty Fogg, president of GLF Farm Services, now Agway. They were the giants of their day. They played key roles in the building of the farm cooperatives that became powerful voices for farmers in the Midwest and across the country.

In creating United Cooperatives, they had put together an enterprise designed to serve thousands of farmers by meeting their needs for quality equipment and materials at the best possible prices. It was a large corporation and my experience in management was largely limited to Cyclone, a company tied together by far more personal, almost family, relationships.

When I submitted my initial budget, I received my first shock. My bosses told me it was not sufficiently detailed and, this was the biggest surprise, far too low. My bosses also told me, in a very nice way, that if I expected to keep my job, I would have to prove my ability by surpassing the sales total for the previous year. Despite my unfamiliarity with the corporate environment in which I found myself, I wasn't discouraged by the sales challenge that had been handed to me. It gave me a tangible goal and, during the eight years I worked for United Cooperatives, sales by my group, the Farm Hardware Department, multiplied many times.

My chief responsibility was the purchasing of farm hardware supplies of all kinds—tools, fencing materials, livestock equipment, electrical and plumbing supplies—a full range of the goods you can see and buy in Farm Bureau stores and in the retail outlets that carry such names as Quality Farm & Fleet and Tractor Supply Corp. Working for me were three or four purchasing agents and all of us were hard-pressed to meet the needs of the hundreds of retail stores that depended on United Cooperatives for many of the products they sold.

Our work was difficult because wartime shortages had created a tremendous postwar demand for all the products needed by farmers and other consumers. Even basic hand tools and household supplies were scarce. So sellers, not buyers, were in the driver's seat. To get the products they needed for their customers, buyers for all kinds of retail outlets were wining and dining manufacturers. The competition was fierce and my United Cooperatives buying staff had to scramble day after day to meet our obligations to our retailers. For two or three years after the end of the war, the supply pipeline was only partly filled and we rarely were able to satisfy retailer and consumer demand.

In addition to heading the buying staff for the Farm Hardware Department, I had other responsibilities. I managed a barn equipment manufacturing plant owned by United Cooperatives. The plant built stanchions, stalls, milking parlors, cattle bowls, barn cleaners and other products used by dairy farmers, beef producers and others in the agricultural industry. I also was the manager of a lawn mower manufacturing plant that produced both reel and rotary mowers. Partly because of my experience with Cyclone and mostly because of my deep-seated desire to make things, I liked manufacturing much better than buying.

As a buyer, I did much traveling and, while it sometimes was demanding in both time and endurance, it gave me an opportunity to meet and know people from all over the United States. I made friends on the West Coast in California, Oregon and Washington, in the East in Maine, Massachusetts, Maryland, Virginia and the Carolinas, and in many of the states in between. Some of my shorter trips were made in the Beechcraft or the Cessna 170 owned by the local airport and made available to United Cooperatives. I also used commercial airlines from time to time, but in those days travel by air wasn't as well accepted as travel by rail.

When I headed east, I often bought a ticket for a roomette in a sleeping car. I could board the train in Alliance, get comfortable in my roomette, and wake up in New York, Philadelphia or Baltimore, or go on to Richmond. When I traveled to the West Coast, a trip I usually made twice a year, I would take a train to Chicago, get a compartment on a sleeper car, and end up on the second morning in Seattle or Portland, San Francisco or Los Angeles. I enjoyed these long train trips. They gave me a chance to see the country, catch up on my reading, and think through some problems that confronted me. Sometimes I was accompanied by another member of the United Cooperatives staff and the trip gave us an opportunity to exchange information and ideas.

A Trip to Remember

It was the summer of 1950, and we were living in Alliance. Our daughter, Caryl, was twelve. My brother Cole, a professor at Michigan State, and his wife, Helen, were free to travel. The company for which I was working, United Cooperatives, had a number of points of distribution in the western part of the United States, some of which I had never visited. I concocted the idea of a vacation/business trip, and so we spent the summer traveling together.

We planned to spend the second night in McCook, Nebraska, but the temperature was over 110 degrees, so we went ahead to Colorado. We were approaching Denver, and there lay the mountains ahead of us. We decided Denver might be cooler so we pushed on and found a nice cool place there. The next stop would be Salt Lake City, but before we got very far out of Denver we were throwing snowballs at each other in the mountains. We included a visit to Dinosaur Park on the way to Salt Lake City. This park dispels all doubt that dinosaurs existed.

Coming down from the mountains overlooking the valley and city of the Great Salt Lake, it is clear why Brigham Young said that this was the place to settle. After conducting business in Salt Lake City, and heading south toward Provo, a friend of mine arranged for us to stay in a cabin at Bryce Canyon, the beautifully colored sculptured canyon. From there we went to Zion Canyon National Park, where we saw the Great White Throne, and then to the Bright Angel Lodge on the rim of the Grand Canyon. Anyone who can look down into that canyon and not feel awed is more dead than alive.

We continued west to San Diego and Los Angeles, making business calls and visiting friends. We moved on up to Fresno, which was even hotter than McCook. But again, nearby were the mountains—the Sierra Nevadas—with the famous national parks, Yosemite, Sequoia, King's Canyon, and Wawona Park—we visited them all. The majesty of the sequoia trees, their size and their age, is awe-inspiring to a tree-lover like me. Sitting on Moro Rock, actually driving through one of the trees in Wawona Park, or staying at the top of Yosemite Falls, I just couldn't keep from exclaiming, "What a world!" Driving from San Francisco north through the Coastal Redwoods to Medford, Oregon and Crater Lake, where we spent the night, we then proceeded to Portland, Oregon. Myra's sister, Lois, lived there many years, and Lois's son, Chuck, shared his expertise at grilling fresh salmon. Lois had brought a giant king crab from Juneau, Alaska, where she worked for the government. It was so big that on a 5' diameter table, its legs extended beyond the edge, and it took two days for the eight of us to eat all of it. I had eaten Dungeness crab in San

Francisco, which I thought was great, but this king crab was really food for a king.

After our time in Portland and Seattle, we traveled east to Spokane, Coeur d'Alene and down the Gallatin Mountain range in Montana, through Yellowstone National Park, which brings back a few memories. Caryl and I had been up to the grocery store, and, walking back to our cabin, we noticed that we were being followed, and not by a person. It was a bear. I told Caryl we would not try to run; we should just walk fast. We did, but he still kept gaining on us, and he was right on our heels when we reached our cottage. I don't think I was ever so happy to see a door. In talking with the people in the grocery store, we learned that he had been in the store, and they had driven him out. They didn't think he was a bad bear, but he was just begging for food. Neither Caryl nor I knew his intentions and weren't sure what it was that he wanted to eat. We were to find out later that bears roamed the park freely. They would come up to a car, put their paws on the door, rub their noses on the window, and if the door was open they would put their head inside the car. The rangers always warned against feeding them, but I don't believe the bears ever got this message, nor did a lot of the tourists visiting the park for the first time. Cole and I caught a lot of cutthroat trout on Lake Yellowstone. We asked the guide to clean them for us, and we took them to the head chef at the Old Faithful Lodge and asked him to prepare them for us for dinner. We gave him a tip, and he did. At dinner that night, our server brought us a platter heaping with fresh trout, resulting in consternation and awe from diners sitting near us. They were so fresh and so delicious. I don't think I've ever had better. Fortunately we had many more than we could eat, and were able to share with the dining room guests sitting around us. Other than the bears, my only word of caution to someone who hasn't visited Yellowstone would be to think twice before walking to the bottom of the canyon, as we did. It's a long way down and even longer coming back up. I also don't think Caryl or Helen would recommend spending a lot of time on horseback, as they did, and were so sore afterwards that they couldn't walk.

On the way home we stopped to see Mt. Rushmore, featuring the great stone faces of four of our presidents, and Wall's Drugstore and the Corn Palace at Mitchell, South Dakota. It was a trip that I shall never forget. I had now seen both the East and West

Coasts of our country. Later I would visit every state in the Union, including Hawaii and Alaska, and Canada from the East to the West Coast. What a world! What beautiful countries I had been privileged to see and enjoy!

My Own Manufacturing Business

Working for United Cooperatives had many advantages, and I was grateful that I had been given an opportunity to increase my knowledge and test my skills in an environment that was much more challenging than I had experienced at Cyclone. Yet, under the surface of my satisfaction, something clearly was happening.

At 3:00 one morning in January 1952, I was awakened by a very compelling thought about my future. Simply put, I realized in a very powerful and personal way that we live in a nation with a free enterprise system where anyone has the right to start a business of any kind. As I lay there in the darkness of early morning, I clearly understood that the time had come for me to start a manufacturing business of my own. I can't say this was the first time I had thought about starting a manufacturing business. I can say it was the first time I had given it serious thought, the first time I felt compelled to take action. I was gripped by the idea. I knew I had to do it. It was almost as if I didn't have any choice in the matter.

At breakfast that day I told Myra and her father, who was visiting us in Alliance, that I was going to resign my job that very day. They were, to put it mildly, surprised. We had never talked about my resigning to create a company of my own. Myra's father recommended that I give my idea more thought before I acted on it by handing in my resignation. Caryl cried because she thought leaving United Cooperatives would mean that she would have to give up her horse. Myra was caught between the advice of her father and the ambition of her husband. She didn't say much but I knew she would support me. She always seemed to have more confidence in me than I had in myself.

As soon as I arrived at work I told my boss, Merritt Crouch, manager of United Cooperatives, that I wanted to quit and start a manufacturing business of my own. Like my family, Merritt was taken aback. When he questioned me about my plans, he learned I really didn't have any. I had nothing definite in mind. I liked working at United Cooperatives. I hated the idea of leaving a community where Myra and I had made many good friends. I also enjoyed working for Merritt. I never had any strained relations with him. He was a very frank and open person. We might get into a hot and heavy argument at times but as I left his office he would always put his arm around me as a way of saying that our differences on an issue would not interfere with our ability to work together.

On that January day in 1952, Merritt was mystified by my decision. He asked, "Howard, why would you want to leave such a good paying job?" When I couldn't come up with any convincing reasons, he smiled and told me he thought I was crazy. I couldn't prove otherwise so I jokingly told him that I was leaving because I was curious to find out whether or not he was paying me enough.

Years later, Merritt and his wife, Vi, visited us in Florida. Myra and I had recently completed a new home and we wanted Merritt and Vi to see it. We parked in the driveway and Merritt carefully surveyed the home. It was large and the front was distinguished by massive columns that, to some, seemed pretentious. After a few minutes, Merritt said, "Well, I guess this proves that I wasn't paying you enough."

In truth I had been paid with more than money at both Cyclone and United Cooperatives. At United Cooperatives, I had been given the opportunity to build on the knowledge gained during my apprenticeship at Cyclone. I learned how to work in the environment created by a large company and for the first time I found myself managing employees who belonged to a union. At Cyclone I had been involved with product development. At United I designed a whole line of poultry equipment and, through working with Follansbee Steel, I gained experience in steel fabrication. I learned more about deep drawing, roll forming, welding and hot galvanizing, and this knowledge of manufacturing processes would prove to be extremely valuable in the days to come.

Mother and Dad

Living in Alliance, I was immersed in my work at United Cooperatives. In fact, both Myra and I were as busy as we had been back in Urbana, when I had many responsibilities at Cyclone and we were both involved in creating the Snack Harbor concept and working to make it a success. Because we were busy and because, in those days, long distance phone calls were so expensive that most people made them only in case of an emergency, we did not stay in close contact with my parents. Looking back, I think I took my parents for granted. They had supported me in every way since I was born, and in my subconscious mind I thought they always would be there. Then my brother Cole called to tell us that mother was seriously ill. She had suffered what appeared to be a stroke while she was at the hardware store. They had taken her home, and I thought the unthinkable—there was a possibility that my mother might be at death's door. We started back to Indiana as soon as possible, and when we arrived I found mother a helpless invalid. Then while we were in Urbana she had a second stroke that was fatal. She was just sixty-three years old.

Maybe all mothers are angels. But I am absolutely sure mine was and I often have regretted that I never told her so. She cared very much about her extended family, her husband and her children. She was an example and an inspiration. She was the one person to whom I could say anything that I thought without fear of embarrassment or reprimand. Through the years she had suffered a lot because of her brothers, Enoch and Loren, who had difficulty accepting responsibility for themselves. Then for nearly twenty years she took care of her mother, who had a leg amputated at age seventy-five and who lived until she was ninety-four. For a number of years mother also provided room and board for her brother, Enoch. In addition to keeping house and making meals, she began to work part-time as a bookkeeper at the hardware store. She enjoyed the bookkeeper role, at least in part because it gave her some relief from her household duties. But it seemed to me that she had taken on too many responsibilities and that they were a little more than she could handle physically.

Mother always thought more about others than about herself. She believed strongly that people of all sorts and in all circumstances deserved to be treated with respect. Often on Sundays, and frequently to the embarrassment of her children, she invited to our dinner table some of the most looked-down-upon people of the community. She had a feeling for people who were less fortunate, and her sense of social justice was far beyond my own. If she thought any of her children were feeling sorry for themselves, she would remind us that a lot of people had far more reason for sorrow than we did.

Like most American mothers she was frightened and depressed by the onset of World War II and the possibility that some of her sons soon would be risking their lives in battle. When my brother Bud enlisted, she sat down and wrote a poem. It is dated December 12, 1941, less than a week after the Japanese attack on Pearl Harbor.

To a Soldier Boy

We can think of a hundred things to say,
Dear Soldier Boy, as you go away,
But we choke them down with a fairy wand
And simply say as we hold your hand,
And smile—"Now, Lad, be good."
Then hoped deep down you understood.
Would that we could have uttered
Some big, strong phrase
That would cling to you for a thousand days!
But our tongues were tied and our hearts so weak
The things we would,
We could not speak.
But they take you, Boy,
When life is best
When you feel the urge of a great conquest.
We see in your eye a little of fear,
A lot of wonder, a bit of a tear.
Though you feel a man and look the part
Life's book of lessons has only a start
And the kind of man you want to be
Is in your hand now to Eternity.
For there's no mother's kind restraining hand,
Nor father's keen eye to understand
To help you through the day.
We go home, crushed, in dark despair,
And cry in our grief
"O God, won't you please be there—
Where we can't go
Where we can't see
Please take my place
By this lad for me."

—*Huldah Brembeck, 1941*

After Mother died, Dad was truly lost. In keeping with his German ancestry, he had a strong sense of duty to family, community and country. His ready, easy smile helped him make friends wherever he went. He had been so successful in politics at the local and state levels that the leaders of the Republican Party wanted him to run for Congress. But he declined the invitation. Since his formal education had ended with sixth grade, he felt he was no match for the lawyers who, then as now, dominated the political process. When he wasn't busy as a farmer, hardware man and political candidate, he found time to sing in a quartet that traveled the area singing at dinners, patriotic rallies and other events. Most of their songs were religious but there were funny ones too. Their singing was so well regarded that they located a professional sound studio in Chicago, where some of their favorite tunes were recorded on 78 RPM albums.

Dad was the kind of person who couldn't live by himself. He needed to be around people. With mother gone, he stayed with Cole and Helen and visited his other children. The year following mother's death, I invited Dad and Cole to accompany me on a business trip through the South. It was February and our car got stuck in deep snow in Raleigh, North Carolina. Then we had to travel over icy roads all the way to Cheraw, South Carolina. When we reached Florida and escaped the signs of winter, we all acted like kids, including Dad.

Here it was still February and we were in our shirtsleeves enjoying freshly squeezed orange juice that cost us only ten cents for a large glass. Soon we were swimming in the Gulf, staying in the Crosley Mansion in Sarasota for ten dollars a night, and eating our fill of fresh, hand-picked oysters. What a life! Heaven on earth—in February! None of us ever got over the experience. Soon we would be coming back and staying, not just a week, but all winter long. As the song goes, "I came to Florida just for a week, but that was twenty-five years ago."

As a young man on the farm, I really didn't get to know Dad. For the most part I worked with hired hands, when we could afford them. Dad was busy with other things. Anyway, boys in their teens aren't too much interested in what their dads tell them. But in the days after mother died, Dad found himself relieved of a lot of responsibilities. He was a different man and so was I. He had more time for his children and we did our best to take advantage

Paul "Bud" Brembeck in uniform, World War II

of it. This wasn't always easy because Dad eventually married again, a woman named Ann Smitter from Grand Rapids, Michigan. She was a very protective wife. But when we did manage to get him away from home, he took advantage of the opportunity to be one of the Brembeck boys. Instead of four, there now were five—Howard, Winston, Cole, Bud and Dad. Once all of us went on a fishing trip to a camp run by Indians on Stone Lake in Wisconsin. We fished for muskie but caught only bass and bluegill. It was such great fun that we talked about doing it again. Unfortunately, before we got around to it, Dad had a fatal stroke. He was about eighty-two.

Having two good parents was a great advantage for all of the Brembeck children. They taught by example as well as by word. I remember Dad telling me to make sure I was right and then go ahead. To illustrate his point, he used what we called a checked field of corn—one with rows that run both east and west and north and south. With its evenly spaced rows, a checked field is easier to cultivate. Dad said, "If you want to end up right, start out right, and that applies to more than planting corn." I'm sure he gave me other words of advice. But those stuck with me and have influenced me to keep looking ahead to see how I was going to come out. If I had not started out right and if I had not checked where I was as I went along, I would have ended up with a crazy looking field of corn that would have been difficult, if not impossible, to cultivate.

Both Mother and Dad often talked about stewardship. They reminded us that all we have has been given to us, that we are only caretakers of what we have, and that we have an obligation to employ or invest our talent and possessions in helping our Lord bring about His heaven on earth. They helped us understand what we should mean when, in the Lord's Prayer, we say "Thy kingdom come." This understanding just might be the greatest inheritance Dad and Mother left to me. As I write this, I am more convinced than ever that we do not make ourselves.

11

Chore-Time

I had promised Merritt Crouch that I would stay on at United Cooperatives for six months to give him time to find a replacement. I kept my promise and on July 1, 1952, I started my new business which I called Chore-Time. I thought that this name would be indicative of the kind of product that I would make. At the time, I had never heard of a corporate mission statement.

Through working for Cyclone and United Cooperatives, I had gained knowledge that served as the foundation for the creation and production of some of Chore-Time's breakthrough products. I didn't know it at the time, but the lessons I was learning would play a major role in equipping me to manage a company of my own. To cite an example of the power of experience, my involvement with Snack Harbor prepared me to recognize the potential of McDonald's. After eating my first McDonald's meal, I could hardly wait to talk to my stockbroker. This was at an early time in McDonald's history and my investment materialized into a small fortune. Had I the imagination of Ray Kroc, the founder of McDonald's, I might have turned Snack Harbor into a billion dollar business.

At the start, Chore-Time was located in our home in Ohio, and the staff consisted of Myra, Caryl and me. The second year we were in business, still in Ohio, we hired Forrest Ramser as sales manager and Kenneth Hagans as engineer. Since Ken had a larger basement than ours, we soon moved Chore-Time's factory from our home to his. At that time, of course, we were more involved in experimentation than in actual production.

Because our family had spent much enjoyable time at Lake Wawasee in Indiana, I decided that Chore-Time's permanent home should be located some place near there. So I picked Milford, Indiana as the location for a factory and, in 1954 rented an old garage building there and moved our business. During this time

Forrest Ramser

Myra and I were using the money we had been saving for many years to build our new home in Goshen. As soon as it was far enough along, we mortgaged it to the hilt so we would have money to operate the business. Myra did the bookkeeping for Chore-Time, and we both worked without taking any pay. In order to have enough money to buy groceries and other necessities, I took a job as a commissioned salesman at Star Tank & Boat Company in Goshen.

Both Forrest and Ken agreed that if and when Chore-Time made enough money, I would be compensated for the six years I worked without pay. Ken wasn't always so generous. In 1958, when Chore-Time was earning a profit and I asked to be put on the payroll at $10,000 a year, he said, "Nobody is worth $10,000 a year." Ken was a loveable person with contrary ideas. About the time Chore-Time started to make money, Ken wanted to be paid off so he could start his own business. Unfortunately that didn't work out. I often would see him at the annual southeastern poultry show in Atlanta, and he never failed to mention that the greatest mistake of his life was quitting Chore-Time. I always agreed. He died in 1992, and I am forever grateful that I learned to know him. He was within a few days of my age.

Chore-Time's original manufacturing building in Milford, 1955.

Aerial view of CTB, Incorporated in Milford today. CTB now includes seven plants in the U.S., five plants in Europe and one plant in South America.

Chore-Time NV in Maldegem, Belgium.

Forrest, however, stood stead-fast with Chore-Time. He received some pay, but it sure wasn't very much—just enough for him and his family to get along.

I'm also grateful to have known Eldon Hostetler. He came to work for us when Chore-Time was still in the old garage building on Main Street

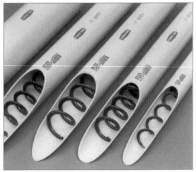

Flex augers

in Milford. Eldon had been born into an Amish family but he never took the vows of the Amish religion. When he joined us, he was an experienced grower of chickens with an assortment of mechanical ideas. He had developed a long-trough poultry waterer that was controlled by a solenoid valve. It was a good product and we made and sold a lot of them. That success prompted me to ask him to work on a new type of mechanical poultry feeder. It would, of course, have to be different and better than the chain feeders which were dominating the market. We had made an auger feeder that distributed feed all right, but it was difficult to make, ship and assemble. It was different but not better.

One night after work Eldon and I were standing on the shipping dock just outside the office. Nearby and ready for shipment were some of these auger feeders. "Eldon," I said, "I think we've come to a dead end. I think we need to back up and start all over again. I know it's impossible, but what we really need to compete with the chain feeder is a one-piece auger."

The next morning Eldon couldn't wait to see me. He was as excited as a little boy. He was carrying a bucket of poultry feed. In it was a tube containing what looked like a flattened wire spring with a tiny handle welded on one end. When he turned the handle the spring revolved, cranking the feed out of the bucket and into another one. What Eldon had created was a centerless auger. He had taken the shaft out of the auger and put the strength of the auger into the flighting, the part that actually conveys the feed. Without the shaft, the auger could be manufactured in one piece in any length. It could be coiled for easy handling and shipping.

Because it was flexible it could go around corners, something an ordinary auger could not do. The new auger consisted of only one piece, contrasting sharply with the chain feeder, which required hundreds of pieces.

The advantages of the new auger were apparent. But I don't think either Eldon or I totally comprehended the significance of the bucket-to-bucket demonstration. It was the birth of the centerless, flexible auger that was destined to change poultry and swine feeding throughout the world.

During the time Eldon worked at Chore-Time we had more fun than the proverbial barrel of monkeys talking about and trying out our ideas for making feeders that were different and better. One of our projects was improving the round pan feeder. It was a venerable product. In fact, Cyclone, the company founded in 1914 by my mother's cousin, Paul Speicher, very possibly was the first company to build and market a sheet metal pan feeder and during my years at Cyclone I had learned much about the manufacture and use of the product.

We were working on the round pan feeder because the trough feeder had a disadvantage. It created a barrier for the birds. So we thought that if we replaced trough feeders with pan feeders we could eliminate the barrier and, according to our figures, feed one-third more birds in the same space. To find out the optimum size and shape of the pan and how it should be attached to an adjustable feed supply tube, Eldon and I spent hours conducting research by sitting in a chicken house studying the behavior of the birds. After experimenting with a number of different ways of attaching the pan to the tube, I asked Larry Meyers, our chief engineer at the time, to produce a pan with a protective, feed conserving grill and to hang the pan on the tube so it would swing without the use of bolts.

The prototype pan feeder had only one problem. It lacked a device that would discourage the birds from roosting on top of the tube. So we ran a wire from a fence charger to within an inch and a half of the auger tube and when a bird flew up and attempted to roost on the tube it would experience an electrical shock and immediately express its surprise in ways that Eldon and I found hilariously funny, perhaps because the reaction seemed very human. It was like seeing a man unknowingly sit on a bumble-bee. Thus was born Chore-Time's Model C which was destined to become the standard poultry feeder for the world.

Working with Eldon Hostetler was always a delight. He and I were brought up very much the same way. Our farm background made it easy for us to communicate. And like me, he had the entrepreneurial spirit in his blood. We made a good team and I would have loved to have had him stay with Chore-Time. But he wanted to do things his way and sometimes this didn't fit in with my goals. So he went on to build a very good business for himself in poultry watering equipment. He located his company in Middlebury, Indiana, and called it Ziggity Systems, Inc. The name came from a nickname Eldon acquired because he liked to sing or whistle a tune entitled "Hot Ziggity."

Like Kenny, Eldon was an original but of a very different kind. He didn't have any qualms about making money or spending it. I can't think of anybody I more enjoyed working with in product development. He had a way of making work fun.

About this time, the late 1950s, the bulk feed truck came into existence, creating more changes in the feeding of poultry and other livestock. Before the bulk feed truck all feed was handled in bags. With bulk feed delivery by truck, which was less expensive, there was a need for bulk feed storage from which feed could be drawn and delivered to automatic feeding systems.

I saw the opportunity for a product that would dovetail nicely with our existing product line, but the boys at Chore-Time weren't interested in making such a thing as a feed bin. I thought of taking the bin-building project to Star Tank & Boat but they were so busy building boats that they, too, weren't interested. Then Arthur Schrock, father of Harold Schrock, came to my rescue. He made it possible for me to build feed bins at night in the Star plant. In consideration of his helpfulness, I incorporated a new company named Brock, a combination of Brembeck and Schrock. Before long Chore-Time moved into a new building on Highway 15 north of Milford and Brock started up operations in the old garage building that had been Chore-Time's home. Then things really started to happen. The Brock feed bin business took off and the auger feeder was rapidly gaining acceptance across America and in many other parts of the world.

Brock

The response to our products in Europe was so positive that we decided to incorporate Chore-Time NV in Maldegem, Belgium. I soon found out that establishing and operating a business in a foreign country is not the same as doing business in the United States. But we kept a tight rein on our new company by limiting our investment to $100,000. If a case could be made for spending additional money, it had to be earned by Chore-Time NV or borrowed from a bank in Belgium. The limitation angered our manager, Max DeCock, but as soon as he realized that we were going to stick to our policy, he stopped objecting and got on with the business of running the company.

In 1960 Helen and Cole, who had been living in Pakistan for a year, invited us to meet them in Athens, Greece on their way home. Cole, who was a professor at Michigan State University, had been working with Mr. Doxiates, the Frank Lloyd Wright of Greece. This was a very interesting meeting for us, for we were invited to have dinner with him at his home, which was on top of his architectural school, on a site we were told he had waited nineteen years to purchase. As we stepped out of the dining room onto the patio, there as big as life was the Parthenon, the most beautiful building of the ancient world. At that time it was still possible to walk through the building, and we later went to a state concert at the base of the building, which made a beautiful backdrop for the concert orchestra. In Rome we stayed at the Hotel Hassler at the top of the Spanish steps, which was part of the Medici buildings. We visited Hadrian's Gate and Villa outside of Rome; also to the north of the city the Tivoli Gardens with the magnificent waterfalls. Then of course we visited St. Peter's Basilica and other places in Rome. One of the highlights of this trip was our stay for about a week at Bürgenstock, Switzerland, high above Lake Luzern, which we were told was just about as near as you can get to heaven on earth. The flowers, the buildings, the service, the food is, as some would say, out of this world. I never did find out what it cost, because my travel agent said, "If I told you, you wouldn't want to stay there. Don't worry— I've covered the cost so you won't recognize it."

At this time the United States, in the eyes of Europeans, was lagging behind Russia in space technology. The Soviets had put up a satellite called "Sputnik." In trying to catch up, the United States had launched a satellite called "Echo," which we were told would be coming right over us one night. When it did, it could be clearly seen, and the orchestra stopped playing. All who were not already standing rose and said, "Long live America . . . long live the United States." We didn't realize it at the time, but we were about the only Americans there—most were Germans, French, Italians, and English. I have never been more proud in my life to be an American. Now it grieves me greatly to see our government's foreign policy destroy this bank of European goodwill.

We knew from the start of our European venture that we needed to build a European management team, and we began searching for someone we could train as an assistant manager. Fortunately, our search led us to an able young Dutchman named Gerard van Rooijen who was completing his MBA work at the University of Oregon. We hired him to join us as soon as he had his degree. He was in training at Milford and living at Lake Wawasee when word came that Max DeCock had suffered a stroke. Although Gerard's Chore-Time training was incomplete, we sent him to Maldegem to assume the manager's responsibilities.

With his farm background and knowledge of poultry, hogs, and farm equipment, Gerard quickly became fully acquainted with our products and manufacturing processes. He was honest, completely open, ambitious, and he liked to make money. As you might expect from the usual stereotype of the Dutch, he was a little stubborn at times but, all in all, he was my kind of man. I have often wished that we could have found someone like him for our operations in the United States.

For the companies I had started, the 1960s and 70s were heady years. For Chore-Time, the flexible auger round pan feeder was fast becoming the feeder of choice. For Brock, the advent of the picker-sheller was creating a huge market for on-farm grain storage bins. Business was good. As I think about it now, it was not just good—it was too good. Chore-Time was selling feeding systems so rapidly that aggressive pursuit of developing its other product lines was neglected. At Brock, grain bins were in such demand that too little attention was given to the feed bins. For me, business was so good that I began to think more about retiring than about continuing to build the business.

To get away from the rush of the business at Milford for a little while and see how things were going at Chore-Time NV, the Belgian business, Myra and I planned a little trip. Instead of flying, we chose the QE2 to go to Europe. To our complete surprise, only a few days before we were to depart we discovered that Andy and Laurie Hardie had booked passage on the same ship and the same sailing. Andy was our minister at the First Presbyterian Church in Goshen. This added a lot of life and interest to our trip. While they were planning to go to London, Myra and I were planning to go to Belgium by way of Paris. Andy came to the rescue and we got off at Cherbourg on the northern coast of France. We hired a car and drove to Paris, where we spent a little time—went to the Lido for example. I had qualms about taking my pastor to the Lido, but I thought, "It's in Paris—why not?" After the experience, his comment was, "Naughty, but nice." He drove us on to our plant in Belgium where we had a good visit with Gerard van Rooijen and his gracious wife, Tillie. I always found Europe very interesting.

It was a very critical time in the history of the two companies, Chore-Time and Brock. Instead of letting the train roll along with the momentum it had gained, I should have been developing more new products and adding more capable individuals to the boards of directors and the management group, including someone who

Paul "Bud" Brembeck at his desk at CTB

could be groomed to succeed me. We needed first-class professional management and we could well afford to pay for it. But we didn't do enough to recruit the people we needed. This, I think, was my first major mistake. It was a case of shortsightedness that contributed to problems that developed later on. But, as they say, hindsight is 20-20.

From the beginning, Chore-Time and Brock were separate companies built on two different formulas. Chore-Time was run more like a democracy. It had a number of shareholders and managers. Brock was more of a dictatorship with very few shareholders and managers. It was owned almost exclusively by Myra, my brother Bud, and me. With fewer shareholders and managers I was able to keep administrative costs at a level that was approximately half that of Chore-Time. As a consequence Brock was much more profitable. This made Chore-Time's managers envious and, although there was no basis for it, suspicious that Brock somehow was benefiting at the expense of Chore-Time. As a matter of fact, the situation was exactly the reverse. Brock was selling feed bins to Chore-Time at a very low price and with considerable benefit to Chore-Time.

To eliminate the jealousy and perhaps reduce some costs, I agreed to create CTB as a holding company for the stock of both Chore-Time and Brock. Putting the two companies together created still another type of corporation for which neither I nor the board of directors were prepared. Creating CTB had the effect of depersonalizing both Chore-Time and Brock. Some key managers started feeling less loyal to the company for which they had been working. They saw CTB as an opportunity to promote their personal ambitions. Many of the goals and policies that built Chore-Time and Brock were forgotten or ignored. The excuse was always the same. The existing goals and policies were too restrictive. They restrained some managers from doing the things they wanted to do. What they actually were doing was moving away from a proven recipe for making money to an experimental recipe which didn't work.

In 1980, at the age of seventy, I thought that I should retire from CTB and let my brother Bud stand in my place. Bud was one of the most conscientious people I have ever known. He was more intuitive and more considerate of others than I was. But one day Bud's doctor called me into his office and told me, "Your brother Paul is suffering from both diabetes and congestive heart failure—usually a fatal combination."

The news distressed me. Bud was ten years younger than I was and I thought of him as my most loyal friend and confidant. I couldn't bring myself to tell him what the doctor had told me. Instead, I allowed him to keep on working—perhaps for my own selfish interests and perhaps because I wanted to be with him as long as I could. As I think about it now, I should have insisted that he step away from the work environment that I think contributed to his early death. I should have urged him to seek other, perhaps more advanced, medical advice that might have prolonged his life. In any event, he died on September 19, 1983, leaving me with both regrets and a powerful sense of personal loss.

At CTB, Paul's death gouged a hole in the management team that was to grow wider and deeper. As the saying goes, when the cat's away, the mice will play. While things were going all right at Brock, they were out of control at Chore-Time. Bud never told me how far out of control Chore-Time was spiraling, perhaps because he was such a kindhearted person that he didn't want to trouble me or get others in trouble. In any event, CTB, once a profitable company with a surplus of money in the bank and a top-notch credit rating was losing money so dramatically that the banks were not willing to approve a loan.

It was obvious that I had made a mistake when I named Jim Evans president. He didn't command the respect of other managers; company politics were being played to the hilt, he allowed others to violate company policies, and business was going to hell. Bud and I had considered the situation and decided that, until we could find a suitable replacement, we should support Jim and remove those most responsible for the losses CTB continued to incur.

Jim was very ambitious to prove himself and it turned out that I made a wise decision by giving him a chance. I did my best to share my knowledge with him and, within a year, we had the company back on track. Within five years, we had made up for our losses and had a surplus of money in the bank. But in the most important area, the board of directors, I had failed to build a team that understood the business or knew how to make money. And, equally important, I had not developed the kind of person I wanted to succeed me. I just hadn't ever thought about the possibility of Bud dying before I did.

I still have some regrets about the way I handled the management of Chore-Time and Brock after creating CTB. These two companies were never the same. The spirit and the loyalty that had been hallmarks in both of these companies disappeared, and were replaced by greed for personal power and money. I had never in my life considered money to be the primary objective. I was still with the company, but my heart was no longer with it. It would have to find another home.

I wanted the person who followed me as president of CTB to share my thoughts and ideas for ensuring its continued growth. That person would also need to be a much better manager than I had been. While the management function always intrigued me and I knew enough about it to know how to make money, I never was comfortable with the responsibilities and restrictions it imposed. So what I wanted for CTB was an experienced, innovative, future-oriented manager who would keep it debt-free, pay good dividends to shareholders, offer attractive profit sharing to employees, and assure that the company remained not necessarily wholly owned by our family, but family controlled.

Business with its risks, problems, and potential rewards had been my life from the time I was a boy. I had created CTB from nothing other than the experience and knowledge that generated ideas. It had become the world leader in its field with its products sold in more than one hundred nations. It had been very profitable, paid substantial dividends, and was considered one of the best employers in the area. When it was at its peak, CTB had as many as one thousand individuals on its payroll.

I retired from CTB on December 31, 1995, and it was only after retirement that I realized that the most profitable return on my life's work was not the factories or the money they created. More likely, it was the quality of employment it provided. After my retirement was announced, I received hundreds of letters and cards from CTB employees. They were thanking me for what I did to make their jobs possible. Many expressed deep gratitude for the way CTB employees were treated, our openness toward employees—our willingness to consider their suggestions and listen to their problems. They also were grateful for the company's benefits, including profit sharing, opportunities for stock ownership, 401K matching programs, health insurance, scholarships for employees' children, contributions toward further education, and the many little things CTB has always done for its employees. For instance, we remembered their birthdays and presented each of them with turkeys at Thanksgiving and hams at Christmas.

As a young man, I had worked as an hourly laborer both on the farm and in the factory. That experience helped me understand how people feel about their employers and why employers should do their best to understand what is important to employees. From our earliest days at Chore-Time, we always tried to be a little ahead of other employers in providing jobs that were rewarding in as many ways as possible. What this involves is really nothing more than doing your best to treat your employees the way you would like to be treated yourself.

On May 21, 1996, CTB employees hosted a reception for Myra and me. This expression of appreciation by the people who helped us build the company was overwhelming to us. It made us feel that we were well paid for the more than six years we worked for Chore-Time without compensation. It prompted us to question whether there is anything more heartwarming than sincere and spontaneous gratitude. I sometimes wonder if people who don't express gratitude—starting with thanking our Creator for everything He has given to us—ever experience real heartfelt joy and love.

I guess all children are beautiful to their parents. That's the way I felt about Chore-Time and Brock. Their products were considered the best in the industry and they achieved a high level of financial success and stability. I loved these children and I was as proud of them as a father could be. Tearing myself away from them was a heart-rending time in my life but it also made me realize how fortunate I was to have been able to create something of value from practically nothing.

Because of my experience on the farm—where in a very physical sense you work hand-in-hand with God—I also felt I was working with the Creator when I started making mechanical products and creating businesses. I was doing things He chose not to do, but which He would be glad to have me do. It surprised me when I realized that most people seemed to think that you go into business just to make money. In fact, I never really thought about it that way. I knew you had to make money to create a business and to stay in business but I also knew that was not the reason for going into business. It was to create something. That gave me the greatest satisfaction. Having made a lot of money, I can say unequivocally that the pleasures that come from making money do not compare to the pleasures of successfully creating something new and beautiful.

One of the greatest joys of my adult life has been creating things. I got a taste of creating new products when I worked at Cyclone. Then I started Snack Harbor and that gave me an opportunity to create a business from scratch. At Snack Harbor, I encountered both problems and opportunities but I also felt a sense of satisfaction in starting a business and making it work. The experience was so successful that I have often thought that, had it not been for World War II, I might have quit my job at Cyclone and made Snack Harbor my primary occupation. We had a good menu, very good food, a very distinctive building, and a good name. With some professional advice on how to package what we had and how to franchise or go public with it, Snack Harbor might have gone a long way.

Through Snack Harbor, I became acquainted with some of the risks involved in doing business. Perhaps taking risks was what made business attractive and thrilling to me. Probably for the same reason, I liked the stock market. Although I never had an appetite for gambling, I did like to play poker because I felt I had as good a chance of winning as I did of losing. And I felt the same way about the stock market. If you invest in good stocks, it isn't a gamble. It's almost a sure recipe for getting rich. Over the years, I've made a lot of money in the stock market and my success was quite a thrill. But I also gave a lot of my stock market earnings away. So I got two bangs out of my buck. What a country! What a life!

Of course, I have made mistakes in life and it never has been easy for me to reconcile myself to them. So I have been obliged to take a long-term view. I have embraced the belief that I never would have accomplished much of anything if I hadn't been willing to take a risk. Consoled by this thought, I'm not so critical of myself. I fully realize that we are not measured by the number of mistakes we make but by how hard we try.

I remember a big mistake we made at Chore-Time back in the early 1980s. Everybody was playing the blame game. No one seemed ready to accept responsibility. I felt so angry that I scribbled a little verse on a scratch pad and passed it around. I was pleased to later discover that at least one person thought enough of it to hang it on the wall of his office.

Lord, if there is blame, let it first fall on me.
If I would have done all I could and should, the problem might not be.
Until I am as perfect as I expect others to be,
Lord, if there is blame, let it first fall on me.

I followed this up later by giving all of our managers a copy of what I called *Characteristics of Good Managers*:

1. Good managers, like champions in any field, measure their performance by their previous best, not by what their competitors do, because there always will be some of them who can't do what the good manager can do.

2. Good managers don't complain, nor do they deal in alibis or excuses. They know their job is to handle problems, even anticipate them.

3. Good managers assume responsibility for their mistakes and those of people reporting to them. They know that the worst mistake is not to admit a mistake and not take action to correct it.

4. Good managers build on the strengths of their company, not its weaknesses.

5. Good managers have respect for their office and know that respect, trust and support are two-way streets.

6. Good managers know the difference between popularity and leadership. They know that making concessions to employees or customers that are not also in the best interest of their company can be disastrous for the company, its employees, its customers and the manager.

7. Good managers compensate their employees on the basis of results measured against stated goals. They reward those who produce and remove those who don't.

8. Good managers know that every person they employ either pushes them up, helping them to become greater than they are, or like a dead weight, pulls them down, making them less than they are.

9. Good managers know that information is of little value if they don't know how to employ it profitably.

10. When they don't know, good managers always ask.

11. Good managers are expediters, not procrastinators, and can be depended upon to do what they say.

12. Good managers, while realizing that making and managing money isn't everything, know it is still the yardstick by which managers are measured.

Characteristics of Good Managers was a more specific and detailed version of the *Rules for Management* that I had put down on paper when we started Chore-Time nearly a half-century before:

1. Build only product that is different and better than your competition's.

2. Do the things that your competition is not doing and that you think are most needed and will be most appreciated.

3. Don't allow scorn or laughter to bother you if you are confident you are doing what is right.

4. Put principle above profit always. In the long run, it pays the best dividends.

5. Create an environment where all employees have the opportunity to do their best work and develop their best selves.

6. The only thing you have to sell is the difference between you and your competition. Be sure you know what this is.

7. Don't be greedy. Profit lies not in the volume of business done but rather in the way it is handled.

8. There is no such thing as small product failure. Little things have a habit of becoming big things.

9. Strive for excellence in all things.

For most of my life, business has been the end and all of my life. But now that I no longer have any connection with CTB, I see things in a different light. I see CTB as a stepping stone to more expressions of my life. CTB made it possible for me to create the Fourth Freedom Forum, a new Oakwood Inn, and the Oakwood Christian Leadership Academy.

Above: This drawing of Howard Brembeck surrounded by Chore-Time, Brock and CTB products and facilities was commissioned by the employees of CTB, Inc. and presented as a gift to Howard. Drawing by Tim McDonald.

12

CTB Products

Since its beginnings with Chore-Time in 1952 and Brock soon after, CTB, Incorporated has become a worldwide leader in poultry feeding, housing and egg collection systems, grain delivery and feed and grain storage systems. Chore-Time and Brock made it possible for me to fulfill other ambitions, such as the creation and development of the Fourth Freedom Forum, the building of the Oakwood Inn and Conference Center, and the robust reestablishment of the Oakwood Leadership Academy, a premier institution to instruct young people in the ways of Christ. Without the success of CTB products worldwide, there would be no Fourth Freedom Forum, there would be no Oakwood Inn, nor would there be an Oakwood Academy.

Howard and Myra Brembeck with his crystal chicken, awarded by coworkers at Chore-Time and Brock in cooperation with the National Broiler Council for sixty years of excellence in all things, presented July 15, 1991.

Chore-Time Flex Auger Feeding Systems

**Chore-Time Egg Production System
with Flex Auger Feeder**

Chore-Time Specializes in Making Cage Systems for Large Egg Producers

Brock is the Leader
in the Development of Feed Storage Systems

Brock is the Industry Leader
in Farm Grain Storage Bins

A Brock Grain Dealer Installation

"I take [great] pride in the development of the Forum. . . . It is becoming known worldwide as perhaps the leading organization dedicated to using incentives and sanctions, the power to give and to withhold, to achieve a world subject to the rule of law."

Photo: South lawn, Fourth Freedom Forum, Goshen, Indiana.

13

Other Ventures

Fourth Freedom Forum

While technically the Fourth Freedom Forum owes its creation to an experience I had in September 1979 while riding on a bus in England, the power that made it possible was the experience that January morning in 1952 when I decided to go into the manufacturing business for myself. Half asleep on that bus in England, I was aroused by a thought that I couldn't get out of my mind. It was at the height of the Cold War with the Soviet Union. Having seen some of the ruins in Europe from World War II, and realizing the devastating nuclear power possessed by the Soviet Union, I thought it would be just a matter of time until the Cold War would get hot and we would all be incinerated. My basic thought was that economic power, not military power, is the power that rules the world. And if Europe and the United States approached the Soviet Union with an economic plan similar to the Marshall Plan, Russia might be willing to forget about going to war. Although still half asleep, I had a vision of Europe and the Soviet Union at peace. This was irrational thinking for that time. Nobody thought that the Berlin Wall would fall, that the Soviet Union would crumble, or that the Cold War would end without a shot being fired. When I awakened I felt compelled, as I had in January 1952, to do something. The thought was so nebulous and so impractical that I tried to forget it.

The only person that gave me any encouragement at all was J. Lawrence Burkholder. For several years I stumbled along with different thoughts. I even created an organization in 1982 which I called the Alternative World Foundation, the precursor of the Fourth Freedom Forum. I did pursue an education in foreign affairs through reading and talking with knowledgeable people. The

Walnut Hill, home of the Fourth Freedom Forum

more I studied, the more I was convinced that economic power exercised through trade incentives and sanctions could achieve goals that could never be reached by the threat or the reality of military action.

In 1985 we named my organization the Fourth Freedom Forum. Its name reflects the principles announced during World War II by President Franklin D. Roosevelt in his speech to Congress in 1941. He stressed that all people had four basic freedoms—freedom of religion, freedom of speech, freedom from want, and *"The fourth is freedom from fear, which translated into world terms, means a worldwide reduction of armaments, to such a point and in such a thorough fashion that no nation will be in a position to commit an act of physical aggression against any neighbor, anywhere in the world."* I wanted the Forum to be a source of objective information on the role of incentives and sanctions in avoiding war and eliminating nuclear and other weapons of mass destruction. With the Forum in place, I spent additional time developing my thoughts on a nonviolent answer to the urgent questions posed by the existence of arsenals bulging with weapons designed to produce indescribable devastation. In 1989, I wrote and published *The Civilized Defense Plan: Security of Na-*

tions through the Power of Trade, a book that outlined my ideas
for rescuing civilized society from dangers that are beyond imagination.

The book proved to be prophetic in some of its insights and
was well received, at least by the minority of people who are
open to new ideas and innovative modes of thinking. In 1998 I
completed a sequel, *In Search of the Fourth Freedom*, which
updated *The Civilized Defense Plan* to conform to the realities
of the post-Soviet world. This book, and a revision completed
in 1999, evoked some flattering comments. President Jimmy
Carter referred to it as "a concrete approach for outlawing nuclear
weapons." George Lee Butler, the U.S. Air Force general who,
before retiring from active duty, commanded all of our nuclear
forces, said, "Howard Brembeck's vision epitomizes the American genius for inspired common sense."

While I was pleased to hear such kind words, I take greater
pride in the development of the Forum. Under the leadership
of its current president, David Cortright, it is becoming known
worldwide as perhaps the leading organization dedicated to
using incentives and sanctions, the power to give and to withhold, to achieve a world subject to the rule of law.

On a far less important level I also take pride in the struc-
ture that serves as the Forum's headquarters. It is a historic
Goshen mansion that we have restored to its original elegance,
tastefully converted for office use, added air conditioning and
the communication facilities required for this age of the
internet, and provided additional space in ways that maintain
the integrity of its architectural design. The mansion majesti-
cally overlooks almost a complete city block in the heart of
Goshen. The lawn is well manicured and the trees are stately.
I love it. No matter what the Fourth Freedom Forum does in
the future, I hope they preserve it.

Goshen

When I was a boy we came up to Wawasee either by the Big
Four Railroad or the inter-urban and changed to the C & O Railroad at Milford Junction. Getting off at Syracuse, we would take
a horse-driven carriage to Oakwood. But sometimes we would

come to Goshen by way of the inter-urban or the railroad. Even as a boy I liked Goshen, and that was a factor in moving my business from Alliance, Ohio to Indiana. Although it was larger than North Manchester, in many ways the two towns were similar. Both were inhabited by conservative, God-fearing, hard-working people who were good custodians of their property.

Moving the business to Milford gave me the opportunity to live in a town I had been admiring. In Martin Manor where only one house had been built, I saw a lot on the bend of the Elkhart River which caused me to exclaim, as Brigham Young had, "This is the place." And so it has been since 1954, when we moved into our new limestone house on the bend in the river. Our first house was in North Manchester on the banks of the Eel River. I have wondered if there was something in my blood that attracted me to rivers, because I was born in Wabash, a river town, and started my first business in Peru on the banks of the Wabash. Perhaps it's just water, because none of these locations excel my suite in the Oakwood Inn on the shore of Lake Wawasee, my favorite spot in Indiana since I was a boy. Today Goshen is twice the size that it was when we moved here. But for me, it still holds its charm. I love our little house with its great white oaks on the river, and the big Fourth Freedom Forum house on the hill with its stately trees and broad lawns. There are many nice things about Goshen but, as Julie Andrews would say, "These are a few of my favorite things." While saying these nice things about Goshen, I must include Milford, which opened its arms to us as a very small company and helped us build it into a very large company with seven manufacturing plants in four states, five in Europe, and one in South America. What a world! What opportunities!

Oakwood Inn and the
Oakwood Christian Leadership Academy

There have been three times in my life when I felt I was told to do something which I had not thought of doing. The first was the dream that awakened me early on a January morning in 1952 that compelled me to create a manufacturing business of my own. The second was the dream in September 1979 while riding a bus in England that compelled me to create an organization designed

The Oakwood Inn and Conference Center

to promote economic power as a viable alternative to the use of military power for solving international conflict. The third time, I was walking along the beach at Lake Wawasee in front of the old Oakwood Hotel. My brother, Cole, had been twisting my arm for over a year to get me to build a new hotel for Oakwood. I had been very much against it, for I felt that the people of Oakwood did not deserve it. If I built it they would not manage or maintain it well; but as I stood there on the beach I got a picture of Oakwood that I had never seen before. Cole and some of the directors assured me that the Oakwood Foundation was operating as a non-denominational organization with no strings to the United Methodist Church other than the mortgage, which could be retired at pleasure. They also consented to the type of hotel I would like. So on June 18, 1994, a meeting was held with some of the Foundation directors, Cole, LeRoy Troyer, representing The Troyer Group architects, and me. It was estimated that the hotel would cost approximately $8 million. But as with my other dreams, everything was very nebulous except the one central thought, which in this case was simply to make Oakwood a little bit of heaven on earth, something we pray for every time we go to church.

Following the building of Oakwood Inn, which cost a lot more than the $8 million estimate, and Cole's demise, which occurred

Oakwood Academy

in June 1996, the dream seemed to take on a life of its own. I knew that Cole wanted more than anything to see the youth camp on the hill restored, which had been a big part of Oakwood under the Evangelical Church, and which had been closed down. Restrictions initiated by the Methodist Church prevented any programs for anyone under seventeen years of age. It was clearly a death sentence for Oakwood. Without young people to replace the older people, Oakwood had no future. While I was not granted the privilege of creating the youth camp, the board did approve the building of cabins and an assembly room for an Oakwood Christian Leadership Academy, a private tax-exempt organization. I hoped that this would open the door to bring young people to Oakwood. I am happy to report that the Oakwood Academy is today a viable institution focusing on teaching young people about Jesus Christ and Him only.

The dream of making Oakwood a little bit of heaven on earth included remodeling the Program Center so that it could accommodate larger groups and make it possible to bring in good quality entertainment and spiritually uplifting talent. We talk about Oakwood being more than just food and lodging, more than just entertainment and recreation. But what is this "more?" Some have likened it to an experience that stays with them the rest of their lives. In thinking about this "more," I came up with what might be a motto or mission statement for Oakwood: *Expressions in*

Christian Living. I was foolish enough to believe that this was probably an original thought until I read Jim Hook's book entitled, *Oakwood's First Century.* After discovering his record of the expressions of ten participants in Oakwood conferences, I couldn't help but feel that this is what Oakwood is all about. It's about offering expressions of gratitude to our Lord for His creation—the beautiful lake, the majestic hill, the park by the waterfront with its giant oak trees.

Cole Brembeck, 1991

Along with this beautiful setting, the restored Oakwood provides a Christian environment where all denominations can gather and worship their Lord Jesus Christ. And they do, at boat church every Sunday morning during the summer.

" . . . all through life you have to keep listening to the wisdom of others and profiting from experience."

14

Reflections

Now that I have attained an above-average lifespan and achieved a certain degree of success, I guess it's normal for people to ask me, "How did you do it?" I never have had a good answer because I really don't know. My guess is that, for at least the first half of your life, success can be attributed to the training and the genes provided by your parents. But all through life you have to keep listening to the wisdom of others and profiting from experience. People often ask, "Weren't you afraid to start your different ventures?" My answer is that I don't think I ever thought about failing. When I committed myself to do something, I naturally assumed that I would stay with it until it became a success.

Ingrained in me by my parents and teachers was a Biblical truth—seek first the kingdom of heaven and the other things you need and want will be given to you. In short, put first things first—don't put the cart before the horse. What is the kingdom of heaven? To me it's more of a state of existence than a specific place in space or time. It's a way of rightful living, doing what you think is right even though this may mean great discomfort or expense for you and disapproval by others.

I know that perceptions change as we move through life. What delights us as children becomes boring when we reach adulthood. What seemed important in midlife seems trivial when we are older and some of the things that were trivial in our middle years take on importance when we are older. For me, there also are some things that have an eternal quality. When I was a boy I loved roaming the woods where I could get a glimpse of wild birds and animals. When I became older, nothing thrilled me more than the majesty of mountains and the grandeur of the great redwood trees. Fortunately, when I was quite young I was able to see much of the eastern United States from the driver's seat of my Model T Ford. When I was older, I wanted to see the rest of the country and I visited every state.

I also spent time in London, Paris, Rome, Athens, Madrid, Lisbon, and other great European cities. I especially loved the art museums. Before I took my first flight to Europe, I had been a frequent visitor to the National Gallery of Art in Washington, D.C. That helped prepare me for my visits to the Reichs Museum in Amsterdam, the Louvre in Paris, the Prado in Madrid, and other spectacular displays of some of the greatest works by many of the world's most famous artists. How could they have created such wonderful work? What genius was in the minds, hands, and hearts of artists who, in many cases, preceded me on this earth by many years? How could so much beauty be open for my inspection and delight?

Now through the wonder of television, I can see great art and listen to the music of the masters without leaving the comfort of my living room. What a world! What an inheritance!

For much of my life, I've wondered what determines the course of events that causes an idea to develop into something tangible, something large and beneficial. Could it be something as simple as faith or what the Bible refers to as "the Word?" Mankind has compiled an amazing list of accomplishments during a brief period of the world's history. People have built cathedrals, skyscrapers, and computers, explored the earth and the heavens, produced astounding works of art, and filled libraries with their knowledge. But no cathedral that I know of compares to the sacredness of Yosemite or Sequoia National Park. No skyscrapers compare with the world's mountains. No mechanism created by mankind is as well designed as the sparrow and no computer even comes close to approaching the power of the human brain. Can we imagine a Creator designing and building a human brain without purpose or plan?

What is this great eternal Plan? Could I be part of it? It's hard to believe that I could be, but even harder to believe that I am not or could not. If not, why was I born and why do I have this longing to be part of the Plan? How could a Creator so loving and so meticulous about creation plant this seed within me without a reason? I can't believe a Creator of such magnitude would not have a plan for a spirit of His creation.

The most exhilarating experience of my life has been the feeling that I am part of something really great—something that reaches beyond the stars, something that makes the stars, a knowledge and an energy surpassing our comprehension that moves with planned precision far beyond the power of imagination.

When I think of these things I can't help saying to myself, "What a God! What a universe! What a world! What a life!" and I am overcome with joy.

Howard and Myra at Elcona Country Club soon after the launching of In Search of the Fourth Freedom, *August 2000.*

Afterword

Reflecting on my past, I had not seriously considered writing about it until Rosalynn Carter admonished me to do it. I have always been future-oriented and have never thought about the past very much. I must admit looking back nearly ninety years has been an enjoyable trip. I recommend it. I also recommend creating for yourself a second life after retiring from your life's work. It may open a whole new world for you.

Myra

While the year of 2000 was, for Myra and me, a year of much happiness and satisfaction, the year of 2001 was to be one of great sorrow, the likes of which I have never experienced. On March 28, Myra died in the hospital in Atlantis, Florida. Being the only girl I had ever loved, and having lived with her in a loving relationship for sixty-seven years, I had never once faced up to the reality of separation and the finality of death, which is the lot of us all. Now that she has departed, I realize how important was her belief in and support of me; when all others doubted me, her loyalty inspired the success of my ventures. We found joy in sharing our thoughts. I still find myself asking her, "What do you think of this?"

Myra was the silent partner of all my business ventures, the wind under my wings, the partner that never promoted herself, a partner I could trust implicitly to tell me the truth as she saw it, a partner with whom I could disagree without the fear of anger. She was a partner who would do what needed to be done regardless of the personal sacrifice, and without complaint. When the manager of Snack Harbor quit, she stepped in and did a superb job of managing the business. When I asked her whether she would be willing to make some real sacrifices in order to help get Chore-Time started, she didn't hesitate to assure me that she would do her best to get along on as little as possible. Had she or I known it would be six years before I would ever draw a paycheck from Chore-Time I don't think there would have ever been a Chore-Time. Had there never been a Chore-Time, there would never have been a CTB, and had there never been a CTB, there never would have been a Fourth Freedom Forum or the kind of Oakwood Inn that exists today, or an Oakwood Academy. Can there be any doubt that it is from dreams and beliefs that all things are made? She was the first bookkeeper and office manager of both Chore-Time and Brock, and had a very low rate of pay or no pay at all for years. While she was hesitant to say much at a board meeting of these companies, her presence had a profound effect on the character of the board. Her good looks, her ladylike conduct and common sense endeared her to employees and customers. She added class, credibility and stature to the businesses that I had created. But Myra's greatest love was family and friends.

Many have told me how blessed I was to have had Myra as my partner for sixty-seven years, and I agree with them. But I wonder if they know or have experienced the kind of love that excels youthful passion and grows each year through the give and take of a long, loving relationship.